PRACTICAL ACTION RESEARCH

for Change

Richard A. Schmuck, Ph.D.

TRAINING AND PUBLISHING, INC.
Arlington Heights, Illinois

Foreword by Robin Fogarty

Practical Action Research for Change

Published by IRI/SkyLight Training and Publishing, Inc.
2626 S. Clearbrook Dr., Arlington Heights, IL 60005
800-348-4474 or 847-290-6600
Fax 847-290-6609
info@iriskylight.com
http://www.iriskylight.com

Creative Director: Robin Fogarty
Managing Editor: Barbara Harold
Editors: Monica Phillips, Amy Kinsman
Type Compositor: Donna Ramirez
Illustration and Cover Designer: David Stockman
Book Designer: Heidi Ray
Production Supervisor: Bob Crump

ISBN 1-57517-041-8
LCCCN: 97-73841

1986C-7-98V
Item Number 1527
06 05 04 03 02 01 00 99 98   15 14 13 12 11 10 9 8 7 6 5 4 3

Dedication

To my intellectual soul mate,
Matthew B. Miles (1926–1996)

Contents

Foreword

Society is always taken by surprise at any new example of commonsense.
—Ralph Waldo Emerson

What makes more sense than teachers embracing the role of reflective practitioners and engaging in practical action research in their classrooms? After all, they are closest to the action in the classroom; they are the most informed about the intricacies of that action; and teachers, along with students, of course, are key stakeholders in any action in the classroom. Why wouldn't it be prudent, logical, and even inevitable that teachers would be reflective about their craft and invested in becoming more skilled in their practice?

As one traces the evolutionary process of staff development over the past thirty years, three phases emerge: Phase 1 "The One-Shot Deal"; Phase 2 "The Spray Paint Method"; and Phase 3 "The Teacher as Researcher." See Figure 1 for the Evolution of Professional Development Opportunities chart.

Evolution of Professional Development Opportunities

Phase 1	Phase 2	Phase 3
"One Shot Deal"	"Spray Paint Method"	"Teacher as Researcher"
District institute day or inservice day	Site-based plans for staff development	Reflective practice through professional inquiry
1970s	1980s	1990s

Figure 1

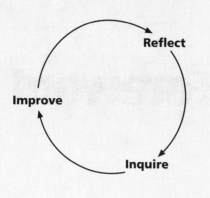

Figure 2

The first phase is characterized by the "one-shot deal," which is comprised of a district institute day or a district inservice day. This day is an opportunity for staff to gather together for a rousing motivational interlude. This earliest phase is followed by a more comprehensive concept of staff development recognized as the "spray paint method." Much as one fixes a room by cleaning it up with a new paint job, this second phase of staff development is often seen as a fix-it-up approach in which staff are exposed to a new look. In this phase site-based teams determine a valued innovation and multiple days and multiple means are designed to ensure "coverage" of all staff with the new idea.

Not to sound too cynical, the "one-shot deal" and the "spray paint method" do offer limited opportunities for teachers to learn and to improve. Yet, current practice is evidenced by this evolution of terminology. Moving from the singular idea of an "inservice day" to the inclusionary term of "staff development," the current, the matured, and the preferred term, "professional development," affirms the teacher as a professional who has a voice in his or her own development.

Embedded in the concept of professional development is the belief that individual teachers, in a continuous and unending cycle, reflect on their own practice, select relevant goals, and choose appropriate inquiry methods to investigate their ideas about the teaching and learning scenarios in their classrooms.

What Richard Schmuck has provided with *Practical Action Research for Change* is a formalized look at the continual process of intense reflection, informed inquiry, and planned improvement (see Figure 2).

Within the pages of this book, Schmuck provides an overarching rationale to justify the role of action research within the arena of academic research. In addition, Schmuck defines and distinguishes between proactive and responsive action research and, in turn, delineates the phases of each.

With this book, teachers and administrators find an invaluable source of practical ideas as they engage in the professional inquiry of reflective practice. With this user-friendly guide, individuals, as well as collaborative and cooperative groups of educators, are given powerful tools to use in their quest for better instruction and enhanced student learning.

In fact, *Practical Action Research for Change* indelibly marks the third phase of the evolutionary march toward school improvement. Through professional development activities of the highest order—personally relevant inquiry, directed by the reflective practitioners—the teacher's voice is heard in the school improvement process. After all, what makes more sense then teachers reflecting upon and inquiring about their own teaching?

—Robin Fogarty
Chicago, June 1997

Preface

The teacher-research movement demonstrates that democratic participation can become a practical reality in twenty-first-century schools. Its growth and vitality prove that social-science methods can become the property of everyone. Systematic data collection and critical analysis can be implemented effectively by nonscientists.

To actualize democratic participation in bureaucratic and hierarchical educational social systems, students, teachers, administrators, and school-based site councils should initiate action research in their classrooms and schools daily, weekly, and monthly.

Action research fosters individual freedom when the process increases everyone's opportunity to search for and to choose voluntarily among alternative actions. Each participant's input is important; everyone must have a voice in effecting action research. The most superb effect of cooperative action research is synergy, in which products of collective thought and problem solving are greater than the sum of efforts of each individual working alone. When action research results in a condition of synergy, every participant's freedom of choice is enhanced.

Action research fosters social equality when participants value partnerships, cross-role cooperation, and cross-generational teams. Each participant's contribution is significant, regardless of age, ethnicity, gender, race, or social position. Another superb effect of cooperative action research is community, where all participants feel valued, included, and productive. When action research results in community, then every participant's social well-being is enhanced.

Educators who participate in the teacher-research movement light a candle for democratic schools. Through the collection of their own data, they listen to the voices of their students. By cooperating with one another, they show appreciation for the contributions of everyone. They believe that action research without democratic heart and soul will not be effective.

—Richard A. Schmuck

IRI/SkyLight Training and Publishing, Inc.

Acknowledgments

I thank the thousands of dedicated educators with whom I have collaborated over the last thirty-five years. I thank in particular the eighty-seven teachers and administrators (forty-five in Eugene, Oregon, and forty-two in Coquitlam, British Columbia) who studied action research with me during the 1996–97 academic year. They read earlier drafts, gave advice for improvements of the content and prose, and offered creative ideas about drawings to make the book's contents more understandable to visual learners. I am especially thankful for the continual intellectual stimulation and affective support of Patricia Schmuck, my colleague, friend, lover, and partner of almost forty years.

Introduction

This book is a helpful guide to teachers, curriculum specialists, counselors, psychologists, school administrators, parents, and students who want to improve their practice by integrating modes of reflection, research methods, and problem solving into their repertoires.

Chapter 1 discusses self-reflective practice; it raises questions about the reflective professional, urges active use of solitary dialogue and a personal journal to enhance the quality of reflectiveness, delineates concerns of the maturing educator, and summarizes the meditative steps of reflective practice used by maturing educators.

Chapter 2 describes how action research differs from traditional research. It presents a conceptual basis of action research, compares two types of social scientists, delineates their differences, and offers a concrete example of a high school English teacher's use of action research in his own classes.

Chapter 3 presents a working definition of action research, emphasizes the importance of group work, introduces the proactive and responsive models, and explains how reflective practice, action research, and problem solving are interrelated.

Chapter 4 introduces the three fundamental phases of action research and data collection.

Chapter 5 explains how to conduct proactive action research, while Chapter 6 does the same for responsive action research.

Chapter 7 introduces the group processes of cooperative action research, while Chapter 8 describes the diverse types of cooperative action research in school districts.

Chapter 9 describes the contributions of thirteen prominent researchers in the history of action research.

An afterword explains how school-based action research has become the teacher-research movement.

There are several opportunities throughout this book for the reader to engage in and reflect on action research. *Practical Action Research for Change* is designed to be used for continuous improvement.

Chapter 1

Reflective Professional Practice

They only babble who practise not reflection. I shall think; and thought is silence.
— *Richard Brinsley Sheridan*

Thought takes place as internal conversation, having developed through social process.
— *George Herbert Mead*

Reflection is thinking about one's own behaviors in the future, the past, or the present. The playwright Sheridan accurately proclaims that "thought is silence"; however, social psychologist George Mead believes that there is an integral association between thinking and social interaction and that thought is a kind of solitary dialogue (Mead 1934).

Reflections of the Future, the Past, and the Present

Educators who do not think about the future cannot contemplate the results of their actions. Educators who do not think about the past cannot ready themselves for change. Educators who do not think about the present cannot understand what to do next. Without solitary dialogue, educators do not know what they truly value.

Educators think about their future behaviors when they plan, design, or rehearse. When

learning to play the trumpet in elementary school, my teacher prodded me to go over the notes and fingering in my mind before I played. In high school, my football coach told us to rehearse offensive plays in our heads before the games. In a college composition course, I was assigned to read, *Think Before You Write* (Leary and Smith 1951), and my college speech instructor urged me to visualize my audience in my mind's eye before walking to the podium.

Now, as a professor, I seldom enter the classroom without at least a skeletal teaching plan, nor do I carry out research or consultation without guiding questions and an explicit design. Indeed, for teachers and students alike, thinking about future behaviors is an essential and necessary stepping stone to effective action. See Figure 1.1 for an example of a teacher reflecting on the future.

Educators also benefit from thinking seriously about their past behaviors—how their behaviors came across to others and what hap-

---

Reflecting on the Future

A teacher is about to meet with the parents of a child who has been difficult to work with during class discussion. She works through the following questions to prepare herself.

What are the disruptive behaviors?

The student does not listen well, often interrupts other students, and is sometimes discourteous to the teacher.

When does the child disrupt the class?

The student is most disruptive after lunch.

What are some possible reactions of the parents?

- I wonder if my child is getting too much sugar at lunch.
- Perhaps my child is too advanced for your class and is bored.
- My child thinks you single her out and pick on her.

How will I respond to each of these reactions?

- Maybe we could alter the student's diet over the next two weeks and see if her social behavior improves.
- Your child's assessment scores in reading and math show that . . . (have assessment scores handy).
- Your child does not seem to have a close friend in class. Can you help me understand that?
- I reprimand your child only when she is disruptive. (Show parents your written record of disturbances.)
- I reward your child at least two or three times a week. (Show parents your written record of rewards.)
- Let's brainstorm together about some new ways we might try to relate to your child.

Figure 1.1

---

pened as a consequence. Serious reflection helps one gain competence, mastery, and understanding, which serve as a foundation of psychological strength when facing the next event or a similar challenge.

Many years after freshman composition, I learned from experience about the power of spontaneous, free writing. I learned to start an article, a chapter, or a proposal by impulsively jotting down words, phrases, and clauses without allowing my pen to leave the paper or my fingers to leave the keyboard. Then, after reflecting on the streams of consciousness in my first jottings, I wrote sentences, paragraphs, and outlines. Later, after more analytical reflection, I prepared drafts, writing–reflecting–rewriting–reflecting–rewriting . . . until I had evolved my voice and was satisfied with my statements.

Also, with regard to thinking about the past, it took me quite a number of years to appreciate the power of debriefing—a term used by diplomats or soldiers when they assess the conduct and results of a mission. Debriefing applies as well

to playing a musical instrument or to participating in athletic competition as it does to making a speech, teaching a class, carrying out research and consultation, or executing a diplomatic mission. In each of those pursuits, serious reflection can help one gain competence, mastery, and understanding. Act first, but think critically about the effect of those actions before acting again! See Figure 1.2 for an example of a teacher reflecting on the past.

The most challenging type of reflection is thinking about one's present behavior, which calls for focusing on the here and now instead of the there and then. Reflecting on the future or past entails segmenting thoughts into distinguishable episodes to consider the interrelated parts. Reflecting on the present, in contrast, calls for moment-to-moment shifts between doing and thinking and thinking and doing.

In his theory about self-concept, Mead conceived of the "I" as a behaving self in spontaneous emission prior to reflection and the "me" as a self that the actor reflects upon. In effect, the

Reflecting on the Past

A teacher thinks about her meetings with parents in the past.

- The last few times I confronted parents about the disruptive behavior of their child, I did not have in mind enough concrete examples of the disruptive behavior.

- The parents saw me as picking on their child. They did not understand how their child's classmates were reacting toward the disruptive behavior.

- I did not connect their child's behavior to the negative effects it was having on other students' learning, nor did I connect it to their child's performance in reading and math.

- I became defensive, and I did not invite the parents to join me in brainstorming alternative actions for each of us to take in trying to change the child's disruptive behavior.

- I do not want to make those same mistakes again.

Figure 1.2

"me" is one's self-perception from moment to moment (Mead 1934). Reflecting on present behavior requires tight coupling between the "I" and the "me." While behaving, the actor simultaneously introspects about the behavior. The behavior and the thinking about the behavior virtually happen at the same time. Reflecting on the present requires one to be acutely sensitive and keenly insightful about the nonverbal messages others emit immediately after expressing one's "I."

I believe that I am best at reflecting on the present when I engage in one-to-one advising, counseling, or conferring. I can monitor the other person's reactions to my actions and quickly regulate what I say or do next according to the instant flicker of insight I get about the other's mental state. As the number of people I simultaneously interact with increases, the difficulties I experience in effectively reflecting on the here and now also increase. I am compelled to reflect more on the past or future rather than the present. Still, as I teach, consult, or convene committee meetings, I strive to remain alert and vigilant to others' reactions to my verbal and nonverbal actions. See Figure 1.3 for an example of a teacher reflecting on the present.

Although reflections on the future, past, and present are very important skills for educators to master, they cannot solve problems. Individuals have a limited capacity to solve complex educational problems with solitary dialogue alone. The

Reflecting on the Present

The teacher meets with the parents of a disruptive student.

She stands as the parents enter the room, aware that she must reach out to them with her right hand while maintaining a broad smile on her face. She invites them to sit down and brings her own chair up close to theirs without a table or desk between them. She searches their faces and physical postures for cues to their comfort and readiness to cooperate. She concentrates on being direct, using only a few sentences, and on maintaining eye contact. Are they looking at her eyes? Do they nod their heads? She looks for pursed lips and listens for sighs of frustration. As she moves the discussion toward cooperative brainstorming of solutions, she is aware of extending her arms out toward them to signal a cooperative discussion. She is aware of using the word "we" several times. As the parents leave she walks with them to the door, again extending her right hand to shake theirs and aware that she has a smile on her face.

Figure 1.3

effectiveness of one's reflections can be significantly enhanced by scientific inquiry—the systematic collection and analysis of data about one's practices.

By employing methods of scientific inquiry, reflective professionals can move beyond their inner selves to engage others in "public dialogue" about the multiple realities that make up classrooms and schools.

Perennial Questions of Reflective Educators

Human beings can think about themselves as a runner in the past, present, and future—one leg is ahead into the future, the other leg behind in the past, the torso poised in the here and now. Yet, as a whole person, the runner moves gracefully from moment to moment toward a goal.

Reflective educators can think like runners when striving to achieve professional goals by pondering questions about their present, past, and future throughout their careers. In the present moment, reflective educators ask themselves, "What am I doing right now? How am I acting? How am I living my values? Are my current actions congruent with my cherished beliefs? Am I practicing what I preach to others? Does my present behavior offer a standard for others to imitate?" Reflective educators help themselves answer these questions, in part, by striving to become more aware of their own self-concepts and their beliefs and values about human nature.

They can grow toward a keener awareness of themselves by writing in a personal journal about the following:

- The central aspects of their self-concept
- The core concepts that guide their explanations of human behavior
- The most important values or desirable ends that guide their professional behavior

Looking to the past, reflective educators ask themselves, "How did I come to be this way? Which of my past experiences affected my beliefs, values, and behaviors? Who were the influential role models of my youth?"

In their personal journals, reflective educators might write about the following:

- Their reasons for wanting to be a teacher
- The characteristics of their favorite teachers
- Influential people in their lives

Zeroing in on the present, reflective educators seek to understand how their current actions affect students, parents, and colleagues. They ask themselves, "How am I coming across to those I serve? What are others' perceptions and feelings about my actions? What are my students learning? How do my students' parents evaluate me as a teacher? How do my professional peers perceive me as a colleague?" Astute reflective educators not only use their journals to speculate about answers to these questions, but they also collect data from others to answer them.

Reflective educators, armed with data from others, become concerned about how they can do things better in the future. They raise questions such as, "What changes might help me achieve my professional goals? How can I increase consistency between my values and my behavior? What changes should I make in my core concepts about human behavior to get ready for future challenges?"

In their personal journals, they might use the following sentence stems:

- As an educator, I prefer to influence people with the following behaviors . . .
- Significant aspects of my vision for education are . . .
- When I apply for a new position in education, I will state the following things about myself to highlight my capacity and values as an effective educator . . .

Figure 1.4 is an excerpt from a reflective educator's journal.

Journal Entry

Reflecting on the Future

The central aspects of my self-concept: *active, athletic, extrovert*

The core concepts that guide my explanations of human behavior: *choosing among alternatives fosters involvements and commitment*

The most important values or desirable ends that guide my professional behavior: *strive to increase students' prosocial skills*

Reflecting on the Past

My reasons for wanting to be a teacher: *to give students of today the wonderful gifts I received from the great teachers who taught me*

The characteristics of my favorite teachers: *caring, clear, supportive, flexible, understanding*

Influential people in my life: *my 12th grade English teacher*

Reflecting on the Present

As an educator, I prefer to influence people with the following behaviors: *active listening, succinct statements, supportive feedback*

Significant aspects of my vision for education are: *cooperative learning and peer tutoring can help develop students' prosocial skills*

When I apply for a new position in education, I will state the following things about myself to highlight my capacity and values as an effective educator: *I adapt my teaching strategies to student learning styles*

Figure 1.4

Reflections Lead to Solitary Dialogue

Shakespeare used soliloquies to reveal the unsettling thoughts of such memorable characters as Hamlet, Lady Macbeth, and King Richard III. Reflective educators can also use soliloquies in their professional practice. This mental activity of solitary dialogue is a conversation between two sides of the inner self.

A typical solitary dialogue is a conversation between one's frustrated past self and one's hopeful future self. The frustrated past self typically uses verbs such as couldn't, defended, didn't, feared, rejected, resisted, struggled, and wanted. The hopeful future self typically uses verbs such as can, search, seek, strive, want, will, and yearn for. Figure 1.5 is an example of a reflective educator working through an inner conflict using solitary dialogue.

Solitary Dialogue

The following is an example of a solitary dialogue with the future and past selves:

PAST SELF: When I felt fear and frustration like this before, I didn't listen carefully to others. I defended myself, jumped to wrong conclusions, and resisted a reasonable compromise.

FUTURE SELF: I will remain cool when under fire. I will strive to listen. I will use paraphrasing and impression checking before seeking to get my own points across. I will try not to project my feelings onto others.

PAST SELF: That's easier said than done. In the heat of anger, I couldn't paraphrase, and when I struggled to check my impressions of others' feelings, I came across as judgmental.

FUTURE SELF: The next time will be different. I am maturing more and more everyday. I will strive to let others know that I do understand and empathize with their feelings even when I disagree with their points of view.

Figure 1.5

Another type of solitary dialogue is a conversation between one's past courageous self and one's future cowardice self. The courageous self typically uses phrases such as bit the bullet and acted, challenged even though I was in the minority, confronted and spoke up, mastered my fear, succeeded in overcoming reluctance and reticence. The cowardice self typically uses phrases such as might fall flat on my face, will forget and leave out important points, will get stage fright and look foolish, won't be accepted and respected by others.

Other types of solitary dialogue are conversations between one's tough and tender selves, task-centered and person-centered selves, pushing and pulling selves, caring and challenging selves, convergent and divergent selves, and productive and reproductive selves.

The Maturing Professional

When educators strive to reflect on their past, present, and future actions and engage in solitary dialogue, their perspectives of work mature. New teachers' thoughts often focus on the insecure self. They focus on worries about survival as a teacher. As neophyte teachers gain experience and reflect on what they hope to achieve, their preoccupation with themselves often diminishes, and they begin to search outside themselves for clues about their students' reactions. Experienced teachers who feel secure become primarily concerned with results.

In *Change in Schools* (1987), educational researchers Gene Hall and Shirley Hord wrote about the concerns of teachers using innovative practices in their classrooms. Hall and Hord's Concerns-Based Adoption Model describes the growth of teachers facing change as growing from concerns about themselves, to concerns about their students' reactions, to concerns about student outcomes. (Figure 1.6 highlights ten Concerns of the Maturing Professional.)

Ten Categories of Maturing Educators' Reflective Practice

Maturing educators are primarily concerned with continuous improvement in achieving results or in reaching valued outcomes. To reach desired outcomes, educators can segment their planning, acting, and evaluating into ten categories, which constitute a conceptual framework for bridging reflective professional practice and action research (Schmuck and Runkel 1994; Schmuck and Schmuck 1997).

Category 1: Set Clear Goals

With thoughtful reflection on their own values and beliefs, mature educators set goals (or targets or objectives) to direct their efforts toward. For example, the educator's goal may be to have students internalize some sort of knowledge or skill, to act in certain new ways, to develop particular values or attitudes, or to view themselves in certain new ways.

Category 2: Assess the Situation

The situation is made up of the people the educator interacts with in the present. In particular, mature educators focus on the current assessment of students' capabilities in relation to the goals set in category 1. They also focus on surrounding social events that are likely to help or hinder students in reaching those goals. While goal setting calls for reflecting into the future, assessing the situation calls for both reflecting in the present and collecting data from others in the present.

Category 3: Create Action Strategies

To move from the present situation toward goal achievement, mature educators use their mental

Concerns of the Maturing Professional

Focus on Self	Focus on Others	Focus on Results
Concern 1: Personal security, status, and comfort *Can I survive in this job?*	*Concern 5:* Others' perceptions of behavior, values, and plans *What are others' perceptions of my professional behavior?*	*Concern 8:* Immediate applicability of teachings *What can others do as a consequence of my having taught them?*
Concern 2: Professional self-esteem *Do I feel good about myself in this job?*	*Concern 6:* Others' attitudes about behavior *What are others' attitudes about my professional behavior?*	*Concern 9:* Future applicability of teachings *What lasting effects have I had on my students?*
Concern 3: Personal values, hopes, aspirations, and plans *Can I make a career in education? Can I achieve my life's goals as an educator?*	*Concern 7:* Effect of behavior on others *What are others' nonverbal and verbal reactions to my professional behavior?*	*Concern 10:* Contribution to society *What long-lasting contributions do my students make to improving our community, nation, and world?*
Concern 4: Professional behavior *Are my professional actions congruent with my values and plans?*		

Figure 1.6

reservoir of knowledge and experience to create effective action strategies. These strategies come in the form of lesson plans, curriculum designs, and intervention tactics. They grow out of creative thought processes that call for reflecting on the past and conducting problem-solving discussions with colleagues and consultants in the present.

Category 4:
Implement Action Plans

The mature educator carries out the action strategies created in category 3, at least on a trial basis.

Category 5:
Monitor One's Own Actions

Monitoring one's own actions involves reflecting on the present. Mature educators strive to make moment-to-moment shifts between doing and thinking and thinking and doing. This requires acute sensitivity to the nonverbal reactions of students.

Category 6:
Assess Others' Reactions

The mature educator collects systematic data about students' perceptions and attitudes toward the processes of the action plans. Such data are amassed using questionnaires, interviews, student journals, and observations.

Category 7:
Evaluate What Others Have Learned

Mature educators focus on whether they have reached their goals: "Have the students developed the qualities sought when the educator set the goals? Are the outcomes or results desirable?" This evaluation involves another collection of data that assesses the knowledge, skills, actions, values, or attitudes of the students.

Category 8:
Confront Oneself with the Results

Compare the desired goals of category 1 and the assessment data of category 7. Look for agreement or disagreement, convergence or divergence, and similarity or differences between the two. Mature educators want to know in what ways they have been effective or ineffective. This self-confrontation facilitates professional growth.

Category 9:
Reflect on What to Do Next

This category is a virtual repeat of category 3: The mature educator once more aims to create an action strategy. This time, the revised plan can be fine-tuned with minor modifications in the original strategy; however, significant changes in the original plan might be desirable. Now is a good time to use the critical and creative ideas of colleagues and to enter into group problem solving about what to do next.

Category 10:
Set New Goals

The educator sets new goals and begins the cycle again.

Reflection, inquiry, and problem solving are ongoing, never-ending procedures. Once new goals are set, mature educators cycle through the original categories again and continue recycling throughout their professional careers. Although these categories of reflective practice appear to be linear steps, maturing educators realize that they can productively start with any one of them. Taken together, these ten categories constitute a mental model for continuous improvement.

Reflective Professional Practice and Action Research

Reflection and action research are two sides on the coin of problem solving. By integrating the two the maturing professional participates in problem solving to achieve continuous improvement.

One way for teachers to integrate reflection with action research is to use Kurt Lewin's (1951) Force-Field Analysis method (see Figure 1.7). According to Lewin, every social situation is in a condition of quasi-equilibrium, a state of balance between actions of opposing forces. As teachers gather data or implement new actions in their classes, they look for helping forces that facilitate

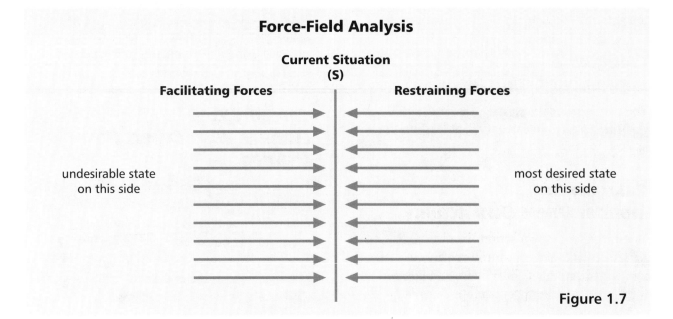

Force-Field Analysis

Current Situation (S)

Facilitating Forces

Restraining Forces

undesirable state on this side

most desired state on this side

Figure 1.7

movement toward their goals and for hindering forces that restrain movement toward their goals.

Maturing teachers find hope in what will facilitate their improvement but are sobered and challenged by obstacles to improvement. Facilitating and restraining forces are the teacher's daily reality in a nutshell. Classroom situations can be improved only by adding facilitating forces or by subtracting restraining forces. Lewin (1951) taught that we ignore restraining forces at our peril. They will defeat us, unless we work hard to reduce their power. Strive to create more facilitating forces, yes, but work even harder to put extra effort into decreasing the power of restraints.

Teachers can also integrate reflection with action research by using Schmuck and Runkel's (1994) STP concepts (see Figure 1.8). In the STP problem-solving paradigm, S stands for the current situation or the state of affairs that exists in the here and now. T stands for the targets one strives to reach in the future. P stands for the path, plan, procedure, project, or proposal that could move one from the current S to the future (Schmuck and Runkel 1994). As teachers collect data or implement alternative practices, they should keep things straight by continuously sorting out what the current situation is, what targets they are moving toward, and what new practices will help them move there.

The Force-Field Analysis and the STP concepts can be dovetailed. Indeed, the current S can be conceived of as a field of helping and hindering forces held in equilibrium. Also, the T can possess positive and negative attributes. The Ps can

search for forces in the social environment that help and hinder their implementation.

Reflection can also be integrated into action research by distinguishing between brainstorming and critical thinking. Brainstorming aids creativity and opens our irrational and intuitive selves. Critical thinking aids in decision making and opens our rational and objective selves. Brainstorming and critical thinking can be executed in any of the steps of action research (see chapter 3 for the steps in action research), in Lewin's Force-Field Analysis, and in Schmuck and Runkel's STP paradigm. Educators must know how to distinguish between them and how best to alternate from one to the other. Students of all ages must also be taught to distinguish between the two and to alternate from one to the other. Brainstorming and critical thinking help bring reflection and action research together into constructive and sensitive problem solving.

Finally, the way to continuous improvement is through self-confrontation. Self-confrontation occurs when people become clear about what they value and gather data to see if they are being true to those values. As discrepancies between values and results of efforts become apparent, there is cognitive dissonance, emotional discomfort, and a wish to change. The sine qua non of action research is clarity of values. To start classroom action research, educators need to get real clear about their core values (Schön 1983, 1987). Then educators can move from focusing on themselves to focusing on results. (See Figure 1.9.)

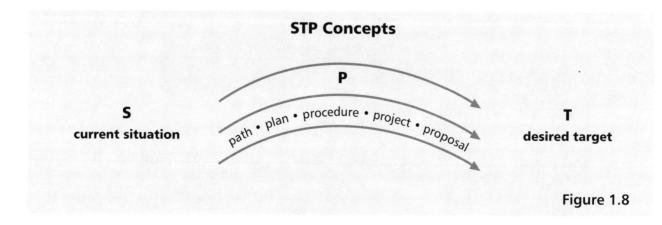

STP Concepts

S
current situation

P
path • plan • procedure • project • proposal

T
desired target

Figure 1.8

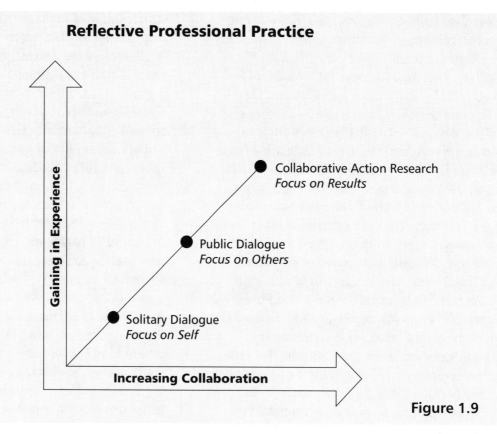

Reflective Professional Practice

(Vertical axis) Gaining in Experience

(Horizontal axis) Increasing Collaboration

Collaborative Action Research
Focus on Results

Public Dialogue
Focus on Others

Solitary Dialogue
Focus on Self

Figure 1.9

IRI/SkyLight Training and Publishing, Inc.

Reflecting

Think of a situation, such as meeting with parents of a problem child, that would benefit from reflection. Then reflect on the future, past, and present to get a clear understanding of the situation.

Reflecting on the future:

Reflecting on the past:

Reflecting on the present:

Journal Entry

Keep a journal of your reflections. Use the following sentence stems to help you reflect.

Reflect on the Future

- The central aspects of my self-concept are . . .

- The core concepts that guide my explanations of human behavior are . . .

- The most important values or desirable ends that guide my professional behavior are . . .

Reflect on the Past

- My reasons for wanting to be a teacher are . . .

- The characteristics of my favorite teachers are . . .

- Influential people in my life are . . .

Reflect on the Present

- As an educator, I prefer to influence people with the following behaviors . . .

- Significant aspects of my vision for education are . . .

- When I apply for a new position in education, I will state the following things about myself to highlight my capacity and values as an effective educator . . .

Solitary Dialogue

Think of a challenge you face. Write a solitary dialogue to get your values and strategies in order. Alternate between your past self and future self or your tough self and your tender self, and so forth.

_____ Self:

_____ Self:

_____ Self:

_____ Self:

_____ Self:

_____ Self:

Ten Categories for Reflective Practice

Think of a challenge you face. List a few ways to carry out the action in each category to get ready to do action research.

Category 1: Set Clear Goals

Category 2: Assess the Situation

Category 3: Create Action Strategies

Category 4: Implement Action Plans

Category 5: Monitor One's Own Actions

Category 6: Assess Others' Reactions

Category 7: Evaluate What Others Have Learned

Category 8: Confront Oneself with the Results

Category 9: Reflect on What to Do Next

Category 10: Set New Goals

Reflections

Reflect on chapter 1 by answering these questions:

1. Do I currently use a form of reflection?

2. How might I use reflection more effectively?

3. How can I make solitary dialogue work for me?

4. What uses do I see for the Force-Field Analysis?

5. How might I use the STP?

6. What are some of my concerns as a maturing professional?

7. How might I use the ten categories of maturing educators' reflective practice?

Chapter 2

Conceptual Bases of Action Research

Every teacher should have some regular and organic ways in which he can participate in controlling aims, methods, and materials of the school.
—*John Dewey*

To have democracy, we must live it day by day.

—*Mary Parker Follett*

John Dewey's and Mary Parker Follett's social-psychological concepts and democratic values have guided social scientists in creating techniques of action research. Dewey taught that society will be more humane, just, and productive as norms and skills to support cooperative problem solving become common in institutions, especially schools. He argued, with emphasis on being practical, that cooperative work in groups should entail participants using research methods of social scientists to solve their own problems. He envisioned teachers doing research in their own classrooms and schools (Dewey 1916).

Follett taught that individual potential is released and contributes more to social improvement as cooperative social relations occur daily in society's workplaces, especially its businesses.

Whereas Frederick Taylor, the originator of scientific management, taught that managers should use time and motion research to impose, topdown, the one best way to carry out industrial work, Follett argued that workers and managers should cooperate as partners in making the workplace more productive and profitable. She envisioned workers empowered to do research on themselves in their own work settings (Follett 1924 and 1940).

Dewey and Follett passionately taught that when participants carry out scientific research on themselves, they create a more self-renewing and democratic social order. Values of equality, freedom, and productivity prevail in concert with one another. Both Dewey and Follett envisioned social scientists giving away their research methods to the people.

Two Types of Social Scientists

Kurt Lewin, called a practical theorist by his biographer, coined the terms field theory and action research; he produced a number of publications about both. As the most influential social psychologist of the first half of the twentieth century, Lewin spawned a large legacy of two types of social scientists: traditional researchers concerned with creating theory and action researchers concerned with solving problems and making improvements (Marrow 1969; Lewin 1951).

The traditional researcher is represented by Leon Festinger, who did laboratory and field experiments to develop theories about cognitive dissonance, reference groups, and social-comparison processes. The action researcher is represented by Ron Lippitt (my mentor), who did naturalistic field studies to develop techniques for planned change, for problem solving, and for training groups. Festinger and Lippitt both used Lewin's field theory in planning their respective research endeavors.

Lewin taught that both types of social scientists can make significant contributions to developing a well-functioning, democratic society. He envisioned researchers like Festinger and Lippitt in a complementary exchange—an era in which traditional and action researchers exchange insights and wisdom. Lewin told his students and coworkers over and over, "There is nothing so practical as a good theory" (Marrow 1969, p. ix).

The Differences Between Action Research and Traditional Research

Educational research can help educators reflect and inquire about their own practice; however, it often does not. Action research, an alternative to traditional research, helps educators reflect on their practice, collect data about their practice, and create alternative ways to improve their practice. Traditional research is usually carried out by disinterested scientists—often with an excessive concern for objectivity and a wish to establish generalized truths. Advocates of action research aim to close the social distance and culture gap between scientist and practitioner and to make research methods useful on a daily basis in the classroom and in the school.

Traditional researchers look at what others are doing and strive not to become personally involved within the study situation. Action researchers look at what they themselves are or should be doing, reflect on what they are thinking and feeling, and seek creative ways to improve how they are behaving. In other words, action research is reflection and inquiry conducted by educators who want to improve their own practice. (See Figures 2.1 and 2.2 for examples of the two types of research.)

Although comparisons of action research and traditional research sound polemical, they are not pitted against each other. Indeed, good synthesis of traditional research can greatly benefit action researchers. Action researchers can use reviews of traditional research along with data from questionnaires, interviews, and observations to guide efforts of continuous improvements. (Figure 2.3 illustrates the synthesis of traditional and action research.)

At least four differences stand out in how Lewin, Festinger, and Lippitt might have characterized the most important differences between action research and traditional research. These differences are illustrated in Figure 2.4.

An Example of Action Research

Robert Hess, a high school English teacher, did action research on writing, which nicely illustrates the four differences between action research and traditional research.

Hess simultaneously served as developer, teacher, observer, questioner, preparer, data collector, and data analyzer. He was sole initiator, detector, and judge. His objective was to improve his writing instruction.

Hess's primary innovation, writer's workshop, offers students a choice in what and how they will write and emphasizes process over product. The teacher acts as a collaborative counselor, moving from student to student for one-on-one help. Students can work together in pairs to help each other to write better.

Traditional Research

A social studies teacher must write a field study to earn a master's degree. He is required to state a research question, review what the research literature says about the question, and collect data in schools other than his own to answer the question. His research question is: Do only children and first borns, compared to later borns, assume more leadership positions in the student government? His literature review reveals a mixed case with a tendency for first borns (but not only children) to take on student leadership positions more often than later borns. The teacher prepares a questionnaire to measure birth order and involvement in student government. He collects data from students at ten high schools in a neighboring county. He writes up the results along with the literature review, research methods, data analysis, and conclusion. In the conclusion he must return to the literature review to show how his study adds to the accumulating literature on the subject. His paper is read by his wife and a colleague and approved by two professors. It is stored in a cabinet at the College of Education.

Figure 2.1

Action Research

A social studies teacher joins a network of teachers doing action research. She is expected to choose a problem in her own classroom or school. She focuses on her school because as a faculty advisor she sees a problem with the student council. She notes that over the last three years fewer students have been volunteering to serve on the council and that more students who do volunteer have been dropping out after only a couple of meetings. She decides to study all students' perceptions and attitudes about the council with a questionnaire. She gets help with the questionnaire from teachers in the network. She collects and analyzes the data; distributes the results to students, faculty, and the administration; and works with an action-research team of council and faculty members to brainstorm ways to improve council functioning. She announces new practices at a faculty meeting and a student assembly and works with the team to implement them. Later, team members interview new council members to see how the new practices are going. At the end of the school year, council members interview a sample of students and faculty members about the council's work. After the teacher reports on the project at a network meeting, a counselor from another school asks her to help him do a similar project.

Figure 2.2

Two Kinds of Research

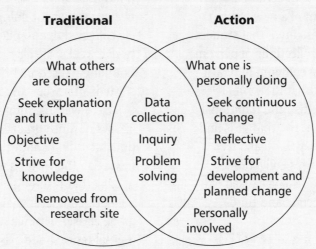

Figure 2.3

Differences Between Action and Traditional Researchers

Improvement versus Explanation	Development versus Knowledge	Perspectives versus Experimentation	Local versus Universal
Action researchers seek a shared understanding of how those who work together affect one another. They are concerned with intervention for continuous improvement.	*Action researchers* wish to foster development and self-renewal of their own group or organization. They are concerned with planned change.	*Action researchers* strive to reach beyond their own, limited points of view by collecting data on multiple perspectives of significant others. They are concerned with obtaining trustworthy information from the right people.	*Action researchers* work by themselves or engage colleagues in self-study and problem solving to increase local effectiveness. They are concerned with building tentative theories to guide future steps in the change and improvement process.
Traditional researchers seek to explain how social relations function, why people influence one another, and what characterizes an effective group or organization. They are concerned with explanation and truth.	*Traditional researchers* seek to build a body of knowledge about social relations that grows over time. They are concerned with accumulation of knowledge.	*Traditional researchers* strive to move outside their subjective realities by collecting data in controlled experiments or field studies. They are concerned with obtaining objective data from a representative sample.	*Traditional researchers* engage other researchers worldwide in studies to build universal theory. They are concerned with establishing generalized principles.

Figure 2.4

Hess began the project with certain assumptions about the development of a new writing program. For instance, he assumed that student-created writing portfolios (collections of personal writings) would be a critical component of a quality writing curriculum, that the writer's workshop method is better than the traditional method of direct instruction, and that girls and boys do not differ in how they think and feel about writing. Interestingly, his collection of observation and questionnaire data caused Hess to question seriously the second and third assumptions.

Hess designed the action research to last twelve weeks. Weeks one to six were spent doing traditional, direct instruction; weeks seven to twelve were spent doing the writer's workshop. He collected open-ended observations during all twelve weeks. He also collected structured questionnaire data three times: before any teaching started, after week six, and after week twelve.

Hess was teaching writing to five other classes of ninth graders at the same time. His understanding about the strengths and weaknesses of the writer's workshop were enhanced by his other teaching experiences. He could not help but compare what occurred in the ninth grade classes with what took place in the experimental tenth grade class. Overall, his experience surprised him. This demonstrates how action

IRI/SkyLight Training and Publishing, Inc.

research offers teachers new perspectives on their teaching practice.

The writer's workshop had more merit than the traditional method in helping to develop favorable student attitudes toward writing and to build student self-confidence with writing. However, the writer's workshop did not achieve what Hess had hoped for in learning outcomes.

During the writer's workshop, students chose to write mostly personal narratives or fragments of poems. Very few tried to write persuasive essays, while even fewer students tried to write expository essays or research papers. In contrast, Hess observed that when he assigned his other ninth grade students persuasive and expository essays, many students did take risks with their writing, reducing their reluctance to broaden the kinds of writing they would try. Hess concluded that the writer's workshop had merit, but some of his traditional procedures helped students learn to write better.

While he did not expect it, Hess also found that girls and boys differed significantly in the questionnaire results. Girls enjoyed writing more than boys and believed more than boys that they could write well. Still, the girls lacked pride in the quality of their written products. The boys were just as proud, if not prouder than the girls, of their written products. His assessment of students' writing portfolios led Hess to conclude that girls actually were better writers than boys.

Hess benefited significantly from the action research. The data helped him grow as a developing English teacher and a maturing professional educator. He concluded that his next year of writing instruction would entail a new integration and synthesis of the writer's workshop and direct instruction. He would also try to become more aware of how girls and boys approach writing differently. He would continue to seek improvement, development, and new perspectives of his own teaching in the local situation.

Two Kinds of Research

Think about your own views about research. Write what you think the advantages and disadvantages are of each kind of research.

Traditional Research

Advantages	Disadvantages

Action Research

Advantages	Disadvantages

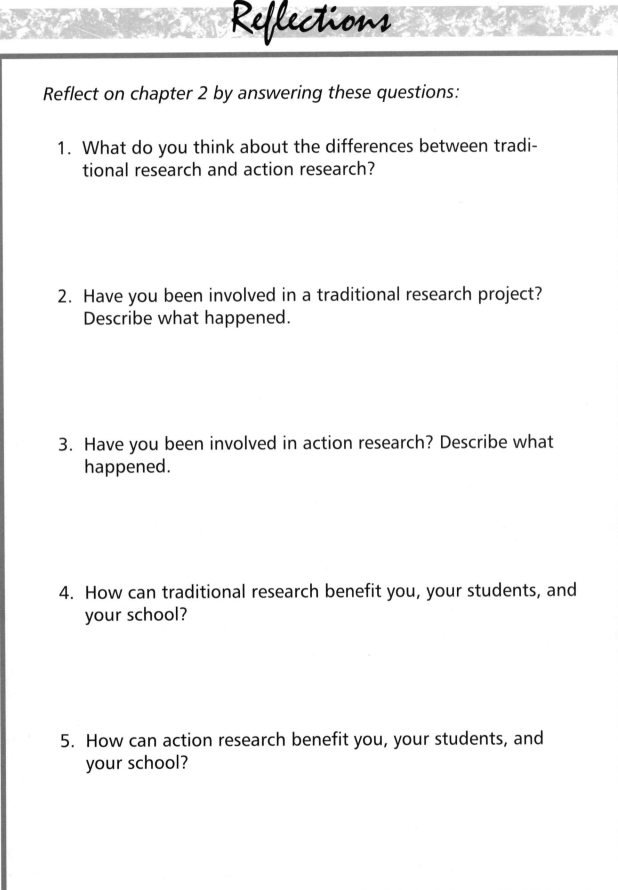

Reflections

Reflect on chapter 2 by answering these questions:

1. What do you think about the differences between traditional research and action research?

2. Have you been involved in a traditional research project? Describe what happened.

3. Have you been involved in action research? Describe what happened.

4. How can traditional research benefit you, your students, and your school?

5. How can action research benefit you, your students, and your school?

Chapter 3

Defining Action Research

Good schools are organic places, always in constructive and sensitive motion.
                                                                        —*Theodore Sizer*

The action of action research . . . implies change in people's lives, and therefore in the system in which they live.
                                                                        —*Jean McNiff*

The organic school that Sizer (1984) writes about will become more and more possible as teachers actively engage in action research. To paraphrase McNiff (1988), true action research involves fundamental transformation of the school culture.

The Need for Action Research

Increasing public pressure for school improvement continues unabated year after year. For at least a generation, the mass media has criticized schools for students' low achievement in language, history, math, and science. Parents have expressed concern for their children's low opportunity for college success because of inadequate preparation in elementary and secondary schools. After more than a decade of vigorous effort in Sizer's (1984) Coalition of Essential Schools, the American public still yearns for excellent senior high schools.

More recently, public schools have come under fire from business leaders for failing to prepare adequately young people in the job-related social skills of group planning, cooperative teamwork, and team problem solving. The ever-blossoming information industry of the twenty-first century promises to put a premium on young adults' capabilities to adapt to unpredictable challenges in a rapidly changing workplace and a cyberspace world. Indeed, knowing how to learn new things, creating brand-new solutions to problems, and working cooperatively with others in new circumstances will become more important than learning specific academic concepts and skills. Soon, the American public might even echo Sizer's hope that schools become "organic places—always in constructive and sensitive motion" (Sizer 1992, p. 142).

Schools will not get into constructive and sensitive motion until administrators, parents, students, and teachers work in concert to fashion classrooms in which learning how to learn,

stretching to be creative, and working cooperatively with others become daily realities. Nor will
schools sustain organic growth without teamwork on everybody's part to examine 1) why they
are doing what they are doing, 2) what they are
doing that is effective or ineffective, 3) where they
want to go, and 4) how they plan to get there.
Reflective practice and action research must
become the hand-in-glove ingredients of an
organic school's repertoire.

Singly and collaboratively, educators should
lead in asking basic value questions about what
their schools should be like, arguing for the
fundamental significance of focusing everyone's
attention on student outcomes, faithfully using
the ten categories of reflective practice (see
chapter 1), and vigorously advocating to gather
data to assess effects of their schools' practices.
They must embrace the action of action research,
seeking continuous improvement in their lives
and in their schools.

A Working Definition of Action Research

Action research is to study a real school situation
with a view to improve the quality of actions and
results within it. It aims also to improve one's
own professional judgment and to give insight
into how better to achieve desirable educational
goals. Action research offers a means for changing from current practice toward better practice.

Ideally, it is continuous and cyclical. Figure 3.1
gives some examples of what action research is like.

Jean McNiff, an experienced secondary school
administrator and author of *Action Research:
Principles and Practice* (1988), exhorts people to
use action research to change their lives and the
systems in which they live. At least two sorts of
change ought to preoccupy today's educators.
The first focuses on educators' theories and
explanations for how students learn. The second
focuses on the effects educators' actual school
practices have on students. Action research
invites educators to test their theories and practices, vis-à-vis student learning, by gathering
empirical evidence to convince themselves that
their current theories and practices need continuous improvement.

Action research helps educators understand
how others—students, parents, and colleagues—
see them and how others are affected by them.
Educators undertake action research to grow
beyond their own solitary dialogues to engage
significant others in "external conversations"
about how the educational process affects them.
Thus, educators use action research to find out
from others, and from assessing outcomes,
whether they should be practicing in a different
manner.

Action research is planned inquiry—a deliberate search for truth, information, or knowledge. It
consists of both self-reflective inquiry, which is
internal and subjective, and inquiry-oriented
practice, which is external and data based. Action

Action research is like . . .

- Looking into a mirror at oneself taking action
- Acting as a detective to uncover clues about the effects of one's work
- Spying on oneself to get the scoop about one's own actions
- Watching a movie of one's self or one's own group in action
- Reading the critics' reviews on the morning after opening night
- Collecting Nielsen ratings on our television program
- Eavesdropping on people's conversations as they leave a play one has presented
- Listening to the judges' ratings during a gymnastics competition

Try brainstorming other appropriate similes or metaphors to action research.

Figure. 3.1

IRI/SkyLight Training and Publishing, Inc.

research is a sort of formal investigation into oneself or into one's own social system.

Action research consists of planned, continuous, and systematic procedures for reflecting on professional practice and for trying out alternative practices to improve outcomes. It unfolds through a spiral of cycles: reflecting, planning, acting, data collecting, analyzing, replanning, acting, data collecting, reflecting; or reflecting, data collecting, analyzing, reflecting, planning, acting, data collecting, reflecting.

As an alternative form of inquiry to traditional social science, action research is the following:

- *Practical.* Insights from data lead to practical improvements in the classroom and in the school during and immediately after the inquiry (e.g., classroom climate, student achievement, and staff morale can be improved).

- *Participative.* Action researchers are coworkers collecting data with and for people focused on a real problem. They are not outside, disinterested experts conducting inquiries on subjects (e.g., they are teachers, students, and administrators in collaboration).

- *Empowering.* All participants can affect and contribute equally to the inquiry (e.g., teachers with students, or administrators with teachers, cooperate as equals in the research process).

- *Interpretive.* Social reality is collaboratively determined by the participants' multiple realities during the inquiry (e.g., students and teachers share their perceptions and attitudes with one another).

- *Tentative.* Inquiries do not result in action researchers coming up with right or wrong answers but rather with tentative solutions based on the multiple and diverse views of participants (e.g., staff members decide to try out new meeting procedures for three months).

- *Critical.* Participants not only search together for practical improvements in

their educational situation, but they also act as self-critical change agents (e.g., teachers asking students for feedback about the strengths and weaknesses of their teaching methods).

Group Work and Action Research

Just as traditional social science can be carried out singly by a researcher (as Margaret Mead [1953] did in observing cultural behavior in New Guinea or Rosabeth Kantor [1983] did in interviewing about work-group processes within Xerox Corporation), action research can also be initiated and coordinated by a single educator. For example, teachers can perform action research in their own classrooms, principals in their own schools, and superintendents in their own districts; however, it would be a mistake to think of action research as being done solo. Action research is participatory and reciprocal. Teachers enlist their students' coparticipation to plan and execute the project, principals engage their faculties, and superintendents involve their staffs or boards. Together, teacher and students, principal and faculty, or superintendent, staff, and school board carry out the action research as partners.

In contrast to the participative and reciprocal norms of action research, traditional social science is often executed within the social arrangement of hierarchical power relationships between expert researchers and their subjects. Notice the word *subject*. The researchers' methods and the evolving role relationship as the research design unfolds put traditional researchers in a position of authority over their subjects. The researcher unilaterally decides what to investigate, who and what to study and for how long, what instructions to present to the subjects, and what to do with the data after they are analyzed. At the end of a traditional research project, only the researcher gets recognition for the research. The researcher often publishes the results in an arcane journal with a turgid style, not immediately useful or accessible to the subjects.

Traditional social science requires researchers to prepare questions or hypotheses and then to collect data that answer the questions or test the hypotheses. An appropriate metaphor is a detective who sets out to identify a criminal. The detective's data collections lead toward reaching a definite conclusion—the identity of the criminal.

Perhaps, this style of highly focused research works most effectively when a clear answer exists to a research question. Usually, the traditional researcher is preoccupied with the research question or the hypothesis, not with the people who are being studied (see Runkel 1978). After all, the people being studied are "subjects" not whole persons. A simile that comes to mind immediately is that traditional researchers are very much like kings associating with their subjects—the people who make up their kingdom. The king does not care who does what for him so long as what he wants done gets done.

Action research, in contrast to traditional research, invites democratic participation and egalitarian collaboration among all members of a particular social setting, whether that setting is a classroom, a school, or a district. Freedom and equality are necessary features of action research. William Foote Whyte (1991), a longtime proponent of action research in agriculture, business, and public administration, called it participatory action research; Richard Sagor (1992), who has applied action research to education, called it collaborative action research. Figure 3.2 outlines some possible Action Research Teams.

Action Research Teams

These action-research ideas are followed by several possible research teams.

Action research . . .	Implemented by . . .
To improve classroom social-emotional climate	• Students and students • Teacher and students • Teacher and parents • Teacher, students, and parents
To evaluate a new curriculum	• Teachers and teachers • Teachers and students • Teachers and parents • Teachers and curriculum specialists
To change report cards	• Administrators and teachers • Administrators, teachers, and students • Administrators, teachers, and staff members • Administrators, teachers, staff members, and parents
To study sexual harassment	• District office personnel and school administrators • District office personnel, school administrators, and teachers • District office personnel, school administrators, teachers, and students • District office personnel, school administrators, teachers, students, parents, and staff members

Figure 3.2

People cooperatively working in groups while inquiring about themselves is a basic value undergirding action research. This is true even when the action research is initiated and coordinated by a single educator. Even the lone teacher or administrator must engage others in the research process; however, the lion's share of action research in education is not initiated and coordinated by an individual working alone. It is often organized from the start as a group effort or team project. Most action research in school districts is executed through teamwork, often by subsystems with such names as climate committees, evaluation groups, planning task forces, or leadership teams.

Because democratic participation and egalitarian cooperation are essential features of action research, those who execute it must have more than just knowledge about reflective practice and scientific inquiry. They should also be capable of executing group-process skills such as communication techniques, joint goal-setting methods, group problem-solving sequences, and consensual decision-making procedures. Action research calls for cooperative group activity in which all participate as equals, share data about one another, and jointly search for solutions to problems or for new ways to reach goals held in common.

Effective action research is democracy in action—especially as the action research fosters group reflection, joint inquiry, shared debriefings, and cooperative action planning. Action research can help administrators, parents, students, teachers, and staff members establish democratic norms, structures, and procedures in classrooms, departments, schools, and districts. It can help establish those good schools that Sizer so aptly called "organic places—always in constructive and sensitive motion" (1992, p. 142).

Proactive vs. Responsive Action Research

The two models of action research—proactive and responsive—differ primarily in when the data are collected and analyzed during the cycle of events. In proactive action research, action precedes data collection and analysis. The educator acts and then studies effects of the actions. In responsive action research, data are collected and analyzed before action is taken. The educator diagnoses the situation, or does a needs assessment, before acting. In both cases, action and research are alternating parts of the same overall project.

Proactive Action Research

In being proactive, educators are inspired to try a new practice. Their inspiration might arise from private reflections on the past, public debriefings swith colleagues or students, or new hopes and aspirations when reflecting on the future. Often, creative inspiration about a new and better practice comes from striving to tighten the coupling between one's values and one's practices. The steps of proactive action research are the following:

1. Try a new practice to have a different effect on others or to bring about better outcomes.

2. Incorporate hopes and concerns into the new practice.

3. Collect data regularly to keep track of the students' reactions and behavioral changes.

4. Check what the data mean.

5. Reflect on alternative ways to behave.

6. Try another new practice. (The sequence has traveled full circle back to step 1. Revisions are made in the original practices to make them more effective.)

See Figure 3.3 for examples of each step of proactive action research.

Responsive Action Research

In responsive action research, educators are careful to collect diagnostic data before they try an innovative practice. Their caution might arise out of their belief that every educational situation

Steps of Proactive Action Research

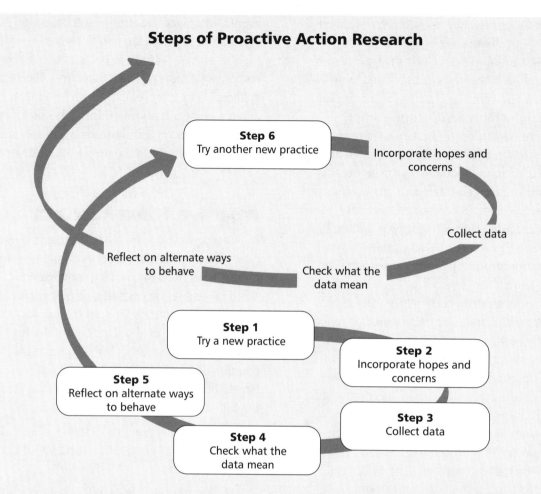

Steps	Examples
1. Try a new practice to have a different effect on others or to bring about better outcomes.	a. A new way to prepare students to work in groups b. A new method to teach some part of the curriculum c. A new procedure to have students assess their own learning
2. Incorporate hopes and concerns into the new practice. Hopes are what one strives to accomplish. Concerns are what one predicts might happen, creating cautionary expectations about the new actions.	Hopes: a. Students will work more diligently together and not "hitch-hike" on the hard work of a few peers. b. Students will work harder and make fewer mistakes. c. The new assessment procedures will lead to portfolio assessments that are meaningful and engaging to students. Concerns: a. Some students will require one-on-one counseling before they are ready to work cooperatively with their peers. b. Some students will be confused with the new method and show their frustration by resisting parts of the new method. c. Some students—particularly those who now get very high grades—might not wish to use portfolio assessment.

(continued on next page)

Figure 3.3

Steps of Proactive Action Research (continued from page 32)

Steps	Examples
3. Collect data regularly to keep track of the students' reactions and behavioral changes.	a. Once a week, the teacher asks students to fill out question-naires about their reactions to group work. The teacher also asks a committee of five students to observe the work groups and give feedback to the class about what it finds. b. The teacher asks a colleague to observe the class while the new method of teaching is being used. The teacher also asks the colleague to keep a journal about the new practice. c. The teacher sends questionnaires to parents about the new assessment procedures. The teacher also interviews a random sample of students about portfolio assessment.
4. Check what the data mean.	a. The teacher holds discussions once a week with the class to analyze the data on group work. b. Colleague-to-colleague exchanges occur regularly about the new teaching method. c. A committee of parents meets to review the new assessment procedures.
5. Reflect on alternative ways to behave.	a. How is what is happening during group work related to what is said about and done with the group work? The teacher writes a solitary dialogue between her caring self and challenging (or confrontational) self. b. How else might the new practice be carried out? The teacher writes a solitary dialogue between her past self and future self about the new practice. c. How can the students be motivated and evaluated? The teacher finishes a sentence stem such as, "As a modern educator, I prefer to motivate students to work hard by emphasizing the following ways of evaluating their academic performance . . . ." The teacher writes a solitary dialogue between her stern self and permissive self.
6. Try another new prac-tice. (The sequence has traveled full circle back to step 1. Revisions are made in the original practices to make them more effective.)	a. In the next group assignment, students start in pairs before creating larger work groups. b. The teacher tries a few of her colleague's suggestions for revising the new teaching method. c. The teacher prepares a one-page explanation of portfolio assessment for parents.

is somehow unique and that it is the professional's responsibility to understand the situation before acting. They might also remember a time when an action they tried backfired because others did not understand the motivation behind it. The steps of responsive action research are the following:

1. Collect data to diagnose the situation.

2. Analyze the data for themes and ideas for action.

3. Distribute the data to others and announce changes that will be tried.

4. Try a new practice to have a different effect on others.

5. Check to see how others are reacting.

6. Collect data to diagnose the situation. (Again, the sequence has circled back to step 1; however, in this second data collection, the general methods previously used will be supplemented with specific questions about the particular issues worked on.)

See Figure 3.4 for examples of each step of responsive action research.

Proactive and Responsive Action Research

Although the two models of action research differ significantly, they differ primarily at start up. Once a continuous cycle of action research is underway, the two models both call for new action and new research followed by more new action and more new research and so forth. Moreover, each model gains in power as it incorporates important aspects of the other. Thus the new practice in step 4 of responsive action research will be strengthened by adding to it a list of hopes and concerns which is called for in step 2 of the proactive model. Conversely, step 5 of proactive action research will be strengthened by adding to it the practice of distributing the data and announcing changes that will be tried (step 3 of the responsive model).

Reflective Practice, Action Research, and Problem Solving

As mentioned earlier, reflective practice and action research are the two sides of the coin of problem solving. The former is problem solving by "thinking through"; philosopher John Dewey (1933) believes thinking and problem solving are one in the same. The latter is problem solving by "studying on"; social psychologist Kurt Lewin (1948) sees action research as a means to solve social problems and to solve the larger problem of maintaining a democracy in a contentious world. Lewin was also the first scholar to use the term action research.

Reflection precedes action research. Start by reflecting on the future and the past. Prepare a solitary dialogue and incorporate into your thinking the Force-Field Analysis (see chapter 1) and the STP concepts (see chapter 1). Then move to action research to gather data, involving students, parents, colleagues, and the principal. As you proceed, strive to reflect on the present. Move effortlessly into problem solving and continue reflecting and carrying out action research as an integral part of your professional practice.

Steps in Problem Solving

In *The Handbook of Organization Development in Schools and Colleges,* Philip Runkel and I lay out the steps of systematic problem solving, drawing on the ideas of Dewey and Lewin (Schmuck and Runkel 1994, ch. 7). The basic idea—one that recurs throughout classical literature on human problem solving—is that a problem is the discrepancy between unsatisfactory present situations and more desirable goals. A problem is being solved as paths are found from the current situation to a future goal. The seven steps of problem solving are the following:

1. *Specify the problem.* A problem is identified when one pinpoints discrepan-

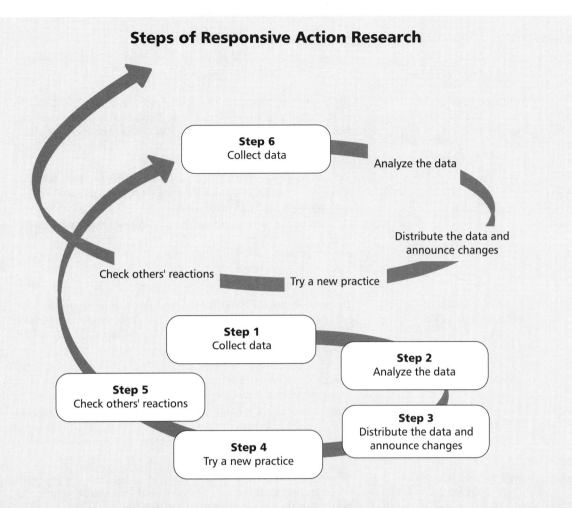

Steps of Responsive Action Research

Step 6
Collect data

Analyze the data

Distribute the data and
announce changes

Check others' reactions   Try a new practice

Step 1
Collect data

Step 2
Analyze the data

Step 5
Check others' reactions

Step 3
Distribute the data and
announce changes

Step 4
Try a new practice

Steps	Examples
1. Collect data to diagnose the situation.	a. A school-climate committee collects questionnaire data from all staff members on their perceptions and feelings about the staff's social-emotional climate. b. Members of a site council interview a random sample of parents about their views on the school's strengths and weaknesses. c. The administrative cabinet uses observations in several behavior settings to assess citizen participation in the school's extracurricular programs.
2. Analyze the data for themes and ideas for action.	a. The school-climate committee notes a large communication gap between the certified faculty and the classified staff. b. The site council concludes that parents tend to be satisfied with the school's math and science offerings but are not pleased with student's writing and speaking skills. c. The administrative cabinet believes that while a considerable number of citizens attend boys' sport events, too few attend girls' sports events.

(continued on next page)

Figure 3.4

IRI/SkyLight Training and Publishing, Inc.

Steps of Responsive Action Research (continued from page 35)

Action Research Step	Examples
3. Distribute the data to others and announce changes that will be tried.	a. The school-climate committee announces its findings at a whole-staff meeting. It tells everyone that it will be running a four-hour workshop for the entire staff in a few weeks. The focus of that workshop will be on improving communication between classroom teachers and other staff members. b. The site council distributes its data back to the teachers and announces it will run a series of small-group discussions with heterogeneous groups of teachers. c. The administrative cabinet presents its data to the staff and PTA. It announces, in both settings, that it will ask for volunteers to participate in an advertising campaign to get more adults to attend girls' sports events.
4. Try a new practice to have a different effect on others.	a. The school-climate committee designs and orchestrates a four-hour workshop for the entire staff. The topic of the workshop is "getting to know our colleagues better—it takes all of us working together to educate our youngsters." b. The site council runs eight discussions for eight different teacher groups of seven each. It concludes with a new task force to work on speaking and writing across the curriculum. c. The administrative cabinet attracts fifteen volunteers (six teachers, seven parents, and two citizens without children in school) to create an advertising campaign for girls' sports events.
5. Check to see how others are reacting.	a. The school-climate committee closely watches to see that certified and classified staff become better acquainted and share information about the school with one another. b. The site council decides to talk informally with the language teachers to give them special encouragement during the change process. c. The administrative cabinet strives to give the fifteen volunteers ample reinforcement and support for their participation in organizing and running the campaign for girls' sports.
6. Collect data to diagnose the situation. (Again, the sequence has circled back to step 1; however, in this second data collection, the general methods previously used will be supplemented with specific questions about the particular issues worked on.)	a. What happened to the communication gap between certified and classified staff members? b. What is going on in the effort to implement a program on speaking and writing across the curriculum? c. What is happening with citizen participation at girls' sports events?

cies between the actual situation and the preferred goals. Two questions guide the process: "What's wrong with the way things are now?" and "What would you like to accomplish that you are not accomplishing now?" An overriding concern is how the present situation falls short of the defined goals.

2. *Assess the situation with the Force-Field Analysis.* Kurt Lewin (1948) conceived of social situations as being held in equilibrium—a state of rest or balance due to the equal action of opposing forces. On the one hand, the situation has helping forces, which can facilitate movement toward a goal; on the other hand, the situation has hindering forces, which can restrain movement toward a goal. The situation is in dynamic equilibrium when the helping and hindering forces are equal in strength. The situation can be changed by either adding helping forces or subtracting hindering forces (Coch and French 1948; Lewin 1948).

3. *Specify multiple solutions.* The purpose of this step in problem solving is to brainstorm as many ideas as possible for either increasing the helping forces or decreasing the hindering forces. The important point is to be creative and inventive. Ronald Lippitt (1949), a protégé of Lewin and my mentor in graduate school, used to say that this stage of problem solving should be exhilarating and inspirational—it is the key to creative planned change.

4. *Plan for action.* In this stage, one tries to be critical and even hard-nosed in selecting only those brainstormed ideas that are feasible and realistic. The action plan that emerges from critical thinking states who will do what when and in what order. This is the plan for change in action research.

5. *Anticipate obstacles.* Before putting the action plan into play, it's important to think carefully about the barriers or hindrances that could arise while the action plan is unfolding. This calls for a second Force-Field Analysis—this time on the action plan itself. After considering forces that might stand in the way of reaching the goal, the action plan is modified so that it has a better chance for effectiveness.

6. *Take action.* The action plan is implemented. Now is the time to reflect in the present; seek tight coupling between the "I" and the "me." This is the action in action research.

7. *Evaluate.* This is one aspect of research in action research. Research is also done in step 2 when collecting data about the force field of the situation. Now, with systematic inquiry into the effects of the action plan, the strengths and shortcomings of the action can be tallied. This process of evaluative inquiry often leads to specifying a new problem, and the problem-solving process is recycled.

Figure 3.5 illustrates a teacher walking through the Seven Steps of Problem Solving.

As John Dewey, Kurt Lewin, and Ron Lippitt saw it, problem solving is continuous—it is the road to improvement, a basic mode of planned change, the professional's way of life. Maturing educators believe that continuous self and system change are the duties of the professional practitioner.

Good reflective practice and effective action research draw on the seven steps of problem solving. In reflection, the maturing educator ponders such questions as, "What's wrong with the way things are now? What would I like to accomplish? What forces in the situation will help or hinder my efforts? What alternative actions might I take to improve the situation? As I act in new ways, what cues can I look for to judge my effectiveness?"

In proactive action research, the maturing educator plans new actions, delineates hopes based on what the actions should accomplish,

Seven Steps of Problem Solving

1. **Specify the Problem.** A high school English teacher thinks that over half of the students do not like to write and do not write well. The target is that all students will like to write and be able to do so reasonably well.

2. **Assess the Situation with the Force-Field Analysis.**

Facilitating Forces	Restraining Forces
Some popular students like to write and can write reasonably well.	Many students spend a lot of time watching TV and do not read much.
I am quite interested in writing and have recently taken two workshops on writing.	I feel unsure about how to change students' attitudes toward writing.
The principal strongly supports my wish that the students write better.	Some of my colleagues do not allocate much time to teaching writing in their classes.
Many parents support my objective of improving students' attitudes and performance in writing.	Only a few students have computers at home.

3. **Specify Multiple Solutions.**

   - Assign students to write about what they watch on TV.
   - Encourage students to take notes on the underlying messages on TV.
   - Seek ways to establish partnerships between students who like to write well and those who don't.
   - Talk with a few colleagues about a small project on writing with our students.
   - See if the principal will help me inspire the students about writing.
   - Check on whether a business organization will donate old computers to my class.

4. **Plan for Action.**

   Next week: Announce to the class that I want to test a new way to teach writing. It will involve writing about TV programs, much like a newspaper reporter does. During class, we will discuss the TV programs we watch and each student will choose one or two to write about.

   The week after: Invite the principal to work on writing with my class, talk with colleagues about a collaborative writing project, and call a few businesses about the availability of computers.

   The week after that: Try to build partnerships between students to facilitate their attitudes toward and achievement in writing.

5. **Anticipate Obstacles.**

   - A few of the good writers do not watch a lot of TV. (I might have to include movies seen at the theater along with TV in the first assignment.)
   - The principal might not have the time to help me. (I should consider getting a few volunteer tutors from the community.)
   - Calling will take a lot of time. (I might see if the school site council will take on that job.)
   - The students won't know how to work as partners. (I will do some training on giving and receiving feedback.)

6. **Take Action.** Implement the action plan.

7. **Evaluate.**

   - Collect questionnaire data from all students.
   - Interview four students who have had difficulty with writing and two students who are good writers.
   - Ask the principal or tutors to collect observation data.

Figure 3.5

specifies concerns by anticipating obstacles, and seeks out ways to evaluate the effects of the new actions.

In responsive action research, the maturing educator collects data about the problem, engages others in analyzing the situation, seeks multiple solutions, takes new action, and again collects data to evaluate results.

Although problem solving, compared to reflective practice and action research, is broader and overarching, good reflective practice and effective action research are miniforms of problem solving. While the three can be conceptually distinguished from one another, in practice they are interrelated and overlapping. Taken together reflective practice and action research are the main ingredients in what Sizer calls constructive and sensitive problem solving. As a single bundle of professional development activities, the three are synonymous with continuous improvement. Figure 3.6 depicts that thinking graphically.

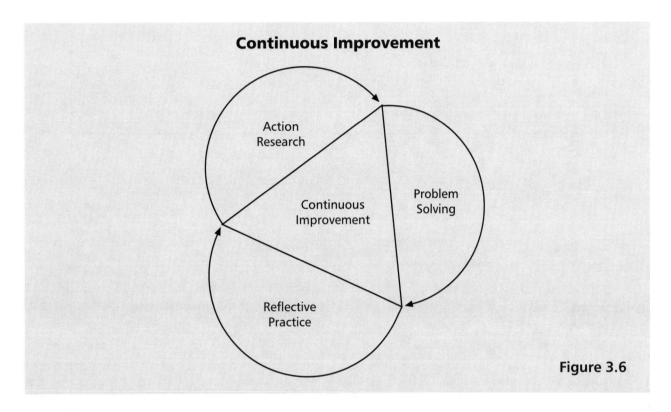

Figure 3.6

Action-Research Teams

Think of some action-research ideas and then brainstorm possible action-research teams.

Action research . . .	Implemented by . . .

Proactive Action Research

Steps	Examples
1. Try a new practice to have a different effect on others or to bring about better outcomes.	
2. Incorporate hopes and concerns into the new practice. Hopes are what one strives to accomplish. Concerns are what one predicts might happen, creating cautionary expectations about the new actions.	
3. Collect data regularly to keep track of the students' reactions and behavioral changes.	

(continued on next page)

Proactive Action Research *(continued from page 41)*

Steps	Examples
4. Check what the data mean.	
5. Reflect on alternative ways to behave.	
6. Try another new practice. (The sequence has traveled full circle back to step 1. Revisions are made in the original practices to make them more effective.)	

Responsive Action Research

Steps	Examples
1. Collect data to diagnose the situation.	
2. Analyze the data for themes and ideas for action.	
3. Distribute the data to others and announce changes that will be tried.	

(continued on next page)

Responsive Action Research (continued from page 43)

Steps	Examples
4. Try a new practice to have a different effect on others.	
5. Check to see how others are reacting.	
6. Collect data to diagnose the situation. (Again, the sequence has circled back to step 1; however, in this second data collection, the general methods previously used will be supplemented with specific questions about the particular issues worked on.)	

Proactive and Responsive Action Research

Think of a creative way in which the two models of action research relate to each other and make an artistic drawing of that relationship.

Problem-Solving Steps

Think of a professional problem you face. Write a few sentences for each of the seven steps.

1. Specify the problem.

2. Assess the situation with the Force-Field Analysis.

3. Specify multiple solutions.

4. Plan for action.

5. Anticipate obstacles.

6. Take action.

7. Evaluate.

Reflections

Reflect on chapter 3 by answering these questions:

1. Do you see issues in your current situation for which you might carry out action research?

2. If you were to do proactive action research, on what new practices might you focus?

3. If you were to do responsive action research, how might you go about collecting diagnostic data?

4. Which do you prefer: proactive or responsive action research? Why?

5. What do you think about the professional goal of continuous improvement?

Chapter 4

Phases of Action Research in the Classroom

*Listen to the voice of the students. They are not afraid to talk about what
actually happens in school.*
—Herbert Kohl

*School should realize democracy as a form of community life by engag-
ing students in joint enterprises sustained by common commitment,
mutual communication, and shared social inquiry.*   *—Emily Robertson*

Herbert Kohl, a high school drama teacher and author of *The Open Classroom* (1969), reminds teachers that students communicate openly with receptive teachers about what happens to them in class and that students can be trusted to speak honestly about their school experiences. Listening to students is essential for teachers carrying out action research in their classrooms (Kohl 1969).

Emily Robertson, a university-based educational philosopher and expert in John Dewey's vision of schooling, paraphrases the democratic rationale for teachers engaging students in shared social inquiry. She explains the fundamental democratic values that undergird teachers and students joining together in cooperative action research within the microsociety of the classroom (Robertson 1992). Herbert Thelen, a devotee of Dewey and Lewin, explained in *The Classroom Society* (1981) that since the classroom group is in itself a microsociety, all participants should contribute to understanding its group processes and participate in all aspects of action research.

When carrying out action research, keep in mind Kohl's ideas about students' voice, Robertson's focus on student-teacher coopera-tion, and Thelen's view of the classroom as "a miniature but complete society" (1981, p. 129). Indeed, students learn how to behave as produc-tive citizens when they partner with their teacher in action research.

Remember that students have the informa-tion teachers need to reflect on their teaching and to plan for change in classroom procedures. Without student learning and development, a teacher has no role to play; without student learning and development, the academic experi-ence has little meaning. Emphasizing student outcomes does not imply that professional colleagues do not render a valuable service by observing one another's teaching. Rather, it proclaims that students' perceptions, concepts, attitudes, values, behaviors, and skills are the primary focuses of data gathering in classroom action research.

Three Phases of Action Research

Three phases of action recur and recycle through all action-research projects: initiation, detection, and judgment. Figure 4.1 illustrates when these phases occur in proactive and responsive action research. Action researchers collect data at each of these phases to understand what they are doing or to reflect on what they should be doing.

Initiation

Initiation calls for action researchers to reflect on the future and inquire about what actions might be taken first. Richard Sagor (1992) refers to this phase as research for action. In *proactive* action research, action is initiated before data collection; therefore, research for action involves reflecting on past experiences, reading literature, and brainstorming with colleagues. In *responsive* action research, data collection precedes action; therefore, research for action entails collecting

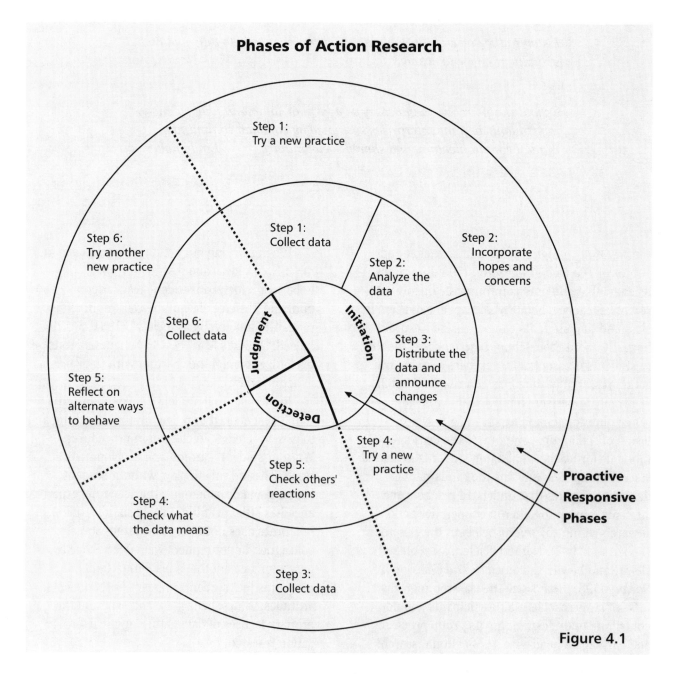

Phases of Action Research

Step 1: Try a new practice

Step 6: Try another new practice

Step 1: Collect data

Step 2: Analyze the data

Step 2: Incorporate hopes and concerns

Step 6: Collect data

Initiation

Step 3: Distribute the data and announce changes

Judgment

Step 5: Reflect on alternate ways to behave

Detection

Step 4: Try a new practice

Step 5: Check others' reactions

Step 4: Check what the data means

Proactive

Responsive

Phases

Step 3: Collect data

Figure 4.1

data through questionnaires, interviews, observations, or documents. Figure 4.2 lists some Examples of Initiation.

Detection

Detection calls for action researchers to monitor and adjust their actions from time to time. Detection requires reflection on the present. Sagor calls this phase research in action. It is quite similar to what Michael Scriven (1980), an expert on program evaluation, calls formative evaluation or what the Lewineans refers to as process analysis during training-group sessions (Bradford, Gibb, and Benne 1964). Figure 4.3 lists some Examples of Detection.

Judgment

In the judgment phase, researchers collect data on the results of their actions over the long haul (e.g., from month to month, semester to semes-

ter, and year to year) and on student outcomes. Sagor calls this phase research of action. It is similar to Scriven's summative evaluation; although, here judgment is executed in behalf of the action research itself, not for policymakers, for which the concept of summative evaluation has often been applied. Judgment entails a kind of reflection on the past; it is systematic inquiry into what has or has not been achieved after testing the actions over a considerable time period.

When collecting data on student outcomes, action researchers seek to judge what Scriven called the *merit* and the *worth* of the results. To achieve merit, a result must have intrinsic value. Gold, for instance, has merit when people perceive it as beautiful and have favorable attitudes toward wearing it. Thus, for Scriven, the merit of a student outcome is measured by the psychological reactions of the students. In classroom action research, teachers assess merit by gathering data about students' subjective responses,

Examples of Initiation

- Searching for and deciding on new curriculum materials
- Diagnosing abilities, attitudes, concepts, feelings, perceptions, and skills of students
- Assessing how comfortable, included, and secure girls and boys (or African

Americans, European Americans, Hispanic Americans, and Native Americans) feel with one another

- Becoming acquainted with multiple parts of students' self concepts
- Introducing an innovative teaching method

Figure 4.2

Examples of Detection

- Interviewing students about their initial reactions to the new curriculum materials
- Observing how students with different abilities, attitudes, concepts, feelings, perceptions, and skills react to different aspects of the class
- Looking for circumstances in which girls and boys (or African Americans,

European Americans, Hispanic Americans, and Native Americans) feel involved or left out of classroom activities

- Observing verbal and nonverbal indicators of high and low student self-esteem
- Collecting questionnaire data once a week on students' perceptions of the innovative teaching method

Figure 4.3

such as their perceptions, concepts, feelings, attitudes, and values.

To achieve worth, a result must have extrinsic value. Gold, for instance, has worth because it can be exchanged for money; thus, one can say that gold is worth about $400 per ounce. The worth of a student outcome for Scriven is measured by the students' performances and subsequent accomplishments. In classroom action research, teachers and students assess worth by gathering data on students' information, skill, and capability of carrying out particular actions. In contrast to focusing on students' attitudes, as when judging merit, worth is often measured by what teachers call tests. Students are tested to see if they have knowledge, skill, or capability (e.g., students can read and comprehend what they have read, students can solve math problems correctly, etc.). Figure 4.4 lists some Examples of Judgment.

Research During Each Phase

Each phase of action research entails research of one sort or another. Initiation calls for either a formal data collection, as in responsive action research, or a more informal retrieval of fresh ideas by reading or conferring with colleagues, as in proactive action research. Detection calls for data collection to track how new actions are working. Judgment calls for data collection to assess results and to revise the action so it will be more effective in reaching desired objectives. Thus, data collection is a formal feature of virtually every aspect of action research. In fact, planned and systematic data collections distinguish action research from other types of professional development.

Data Collection

Action research requires a planned method for gathering data. The most popular ways to collect data are questionnaires, interviews, observations, and documents.

Questionnaires

Questionnaires are printed lists of interrogative or declarative statements that individuals respond to

Examples of Judgment

Judging Merit	Judging Worth
• Assessing students' attitudes toward different parts of the new curriculum materials	• Testing students' recall and understanding of high points in the new curriculum materials
• Measuring how students with different abilities, attitudes, concepts, feelings, perceptions, and skills value different aspects of the class	• Observing how much students with different abilities, attitudes, concepts, feelings, perceptions, and skills stick with the tasks of different aspects of classroom work
• Assessing girls' and boys' (or African Americans', European Americans', Hispanic Americans', and Native Americans') feelings of acceptance or alienation toward different classroom activities	• Observing how often girls and boys (or African Americans, European Americans, Hispanic Americans, and Native Americans) perform task and social-emotional roles during cooperative group projects
• Measuring students' academic self-esteem in relation to language arts, science, math, social studies, etc.	• Testing students' understanding of academic subjects, such as language arts, science, math, social studies, etc.
• Assessing students' attitudes toward different aspects of the new teaching method	• Testing how well students apply what they have learned from a new teaching method to the solution of a community problem

Figure 4.4

in writing. Individuals normally fill out questionnaires privately, but groups can be asked to respond to a questionnaire via discussion and polling. Questionnaires can be simple or complex and be open-ended or have rating scales. Questionnaires are the most useful to do the following:

- Announce the beginning of a responsive action-research project

- Understand students' subjective states, perceptions, ideas, feelings, cognitions, attitudes, and values

- Have all students respond to the same statements at the same time

- Collect a great deal of data in a short amount of time

- Allow students to remain anonymous to the data collector and analyst

Simple open-ended questionnaires can be created easily and quickly. The data collector does not need to give a lengthy explanation of the questionnaire, and students can usually complete them quickly. When analyzing simple-open ended questions, the data often reveal unexpected thoughts and feelings from the students. Such data supply a rich array of quotations for feedback.

Simple open-ended questions can be proffered with a little more complexity and structure, if they ask students to write, for instance, three things about the class that help their learning and three things about the class that get in the way of their learning. By doing that, teachers improve their chance to obtain unexpected thoughts or feelings and a few rich quotations, because with this method every student is prodded to write six answers. In a class of 25, up to 150 answers could be obtained for the analysis. Furthermore, the addition of such structure stimulates students to think deeply about their answers and to go beyond superficial clichés.

However helpful open-ended questions are, they do have some disadvantages. Teachers may find that some of the responses are ambiguous, that different words sometimes have the same meaning or that same words sometimes have different meanings. Analyzing the responses can also be time consuming.

Any disadvantages associated with open-ended questions can be avoided by using rating scales. Specific statements with rating scales can be used to learn about specific aspects of the class. They can also be answered and tallied quickly. Rating scales also make it easier to clearly portray the information in tables or figures for feedback sessions.

Structured questionnaires with rating scales can be presented with bipolar words at both ends of the scale and numbers in between. For example, I like to work on cooperative projects in this class: Agree 1, 2, 3, 4, 5, 6 Disagree; or, I feel friendly toward my teacher in this class: Always 1, 2, 3 Never.

In complex questionnaires with lists of statements accompanied by rating scales, it's important that every individual statement focuses on one item. Keep the rating scale consistent throughout. Unexpected or rich responses can be gained by adding a few open-ended questions at the end of a complex and structured questionnaire. For example, Write about three things you do not want changed in this class and three things you would like changed. Figure 4.5 highlights the Advantages vs. Disadvantages of Questionnaires.

Interviews

Interviews are conversations in which interviewers pose questions to interviewees. They can be held with individuals, one-on-one, or with groups, as in focus-group interviews in which a group is asked to discuss a particular topic in the presence of an interviewer, perhaps with an audio or video recorder. Interviews can vary in how formal or informal they are. Interviews are useful in the following situations:

- Establish rapport and closeness while collecting data

- Probe into students' subjective states about the class

Advantages vs. Disadvantages of Questionnaires

Advantages	Disadvantages
• Open-ended questions can be created easily and quickly	• Open-ended responses can be ambiguous
• Respondents can complete them quickly	• Analysis of open-ended responses takes time
• Open-ended responses offer rich quotations that are useful for data feedback	• If questions with rating scales include two or more ideas, the results will be unclear
• The chance of learning unexpected things is improved by asking for a few responses to the same question	• The data collector cannot ask respondents to clarify their answers
• Questions with rating scales can be scored quickly, and results can be clearly presented in graphic tables and figures	• The data collector has little opportunity to establish trust and rapport with the respondents

Figure 4.5

• Obtain information from students who cannot easily write about their thoughts and feelings

• Use students' remarks to stimulate oral contributions from other students

Interviews start with broad and open-ended questions, such as "Tell me how you feel about this class," and gradually flow, in the shape of a funnel, toward more pointed and specific questions, such as "Tell me how you reacted to our discussion about *Romeo and Juliet*."

Interviews should follow a preplanned format, especially if answers will be compared across individuals or small groups. Interviews should also afford time for "sidetracking." Interviewers use probes to elicit richer data: "Tell me more about that. Can you give me an example of that? What, in particular, are you thinking about there? How were you feeling at that time?"

Interviews tend to be time consuming, so it's important for teachers to use interviews as a natural and integral part of teaching. It's best to use interviews during informal times (before class, in passing, at lunch, or after school) or during relaxed times with everyone in the class. Some students may be reluctant to give answers in an interview because they may fear that what

they say will be used against them. To avoid this, it's a good idea to have students pool their responses in small groups before they offer them as data. This allows individuals' responses to remain anonymous. Figure 4.6 highlights the Advantages vs. Disadvantages of Interviews.

Observations

Observations involve attentively watching and systematically recording what is seen and heard. They can vary in how structured or unstructured the observer's categories are when making a record of the observations. Video recorders are useful for collecting observation data. Observations are useful in the following situations:

• Check for nonverbal expressions of students' feelings

• See which students play together, walk together between classes, and sit together at lunch, assemblies, or extracurricular events

• Grasp how students communicate with one another during group discussions

• Check for how much time particular students spend on particular tasks

Advantages vs. Disadvantages of Interviews

Advantages	Disadvantages
• The data collector can probe for clarification and elaboration	• Time consuming
• The data collector can build rapport and closeness with respondents	• Challenge of sampling when everyone can't be interviewed
• Can help in collecting data from respondents who cannot or will not write about their thoughts and feelings	• Lack of respondents' anonymity
• Respondents are anonymous when they pool answers outside earshot of the data collector	• The data collector's physical characteristics and social position may lead to bias in respondents' answers
• Data can be gathered via audiotapes	• Respondents may fear that what they say will be used against them

Figure 4.6

• Understand how a teacher communicates with students with different characteristics at different times

Observations vary in how structured or unstructured the observer's categories are. There is not time to do structured observation while teaching. Most observations will be unstructured or semistructured. Observations, nevertheless, are critical during step 3 in proactive action research and step 5 in responsive action research (see chapter 3 for the steps of proactive and responsive research). During those steps, teachers need to be sensitive to how students react to the new

practices. Structured observations can be used in at least three ways during action research:

1. To train students to observe specific things during particular time periods

2. To have older students who are tutors, helpers, or assistants make structured observations of the new practices

3. To enlist a colleague's help or to have the principal watch for specific things during an observation period.

Figure 4.7 highlights the Advantages vs. Disadvantages of Observations.

Advantages vs. Disadvantages of Observations

Advantages	Disadvantages
• Can gather data about behaviors, rather than just perceptions and feelings	• The data collector's presence can alter the respondents' behavior
• Can see things that some respondents will not be able to report	• The data collectors might have to wait a long time before seeing what they seek to observe
• Data can be gathered via video	• Different data collectors might see different things while observing the same events

Figure 4.7

Documents

Documents are public records, press clippings, and private journals and diaries. Action researchers use an analytical procedure called content analysis to analyze the documents for recurring themes and for multiple meanings. Curriculum materials, textbooks, and instructional strategies also can be analyzed to understand the themes and meanings that are being presented to students. Figure 4.8 highlights the Advantages vs. Disadvantages of Documents.

Data Collection for Action Research

Every action-research project should include its own unique mix of questionnaires, interviews, observations, and documents. It is each teacher's challenge to create his or her own special package of the four methods. To learn more about data collection, see *Doing Research: A Handbook for Teachers,* by Rob Walker (1985).

Advantages vs. Disadvantages of Documents

Advantages	Disadvantages
• Data are unaffected by the data collector's presence	• Records might be incomplete or amassed in biased ways
• Historical events can be studied objectively	• Difficult to check on the validity of the information

Figure 4.8

Phases of Action Research

Think of a professional problem you are facing, you faced in the past, or you may face in the future. Jot down some possible reflections or actions for each of the phases.

Initiation

Detection

Judgment (merit and worth)

Data Collecting
Past, Present, and Future

Reflect on how you have collected data in the past, how you are currently collecting data, and how you might want to collect data in the future.

Questionnaires

    Past:

    Present:

    Future:

Interviews

    Past:

    Present:

    Future:

Observations

    Past:

    Present:

    Future:

Documents

    Past:

    Present:

    Future:

Reflections

Reflect on chapter 4 by answering these questions:

1. When you initiate a new project or new technique, what data-collection methods do you prefer to use?

2. When you wish to detect how one of your projects or techniques is working, what data-collection methods do you prefer to use?

3. When you want to judge whether your projects or techniques are getting the results you want, what data-collection methods do you prefer to use?

4. What more do you need to learn about data collection for you to feel comfortable carrying out an action-research project?

Chapter 5

Proactive Action Research

*If you have built castles in the air, your work need not be lost, there is
where they should be. Now put foundations under them.*
                                                    —Henry David Thoreau

*I tried the writer's workshop with tenth graders to give them more choice
and freedom in what and how they write and to help them become more
effective writers.*
                                                    —Robert Hess

Hess's action research was proactive because his main action idea, writer's workshop for tenth graders (see chapter 2), grew out of his own reflections from professional reading and classroom experiences. He believed that his traditional method of direct instruction in writing was not helping students develop favorable attitudes toward writing, nor was it helping them build self-confidence as writers. Instead, he thought that more and more of his students were turned off to writing and that it was time to try another teaching method.

Marilyn Lund, a new teacher, and James Johnson, a mature teacher, both realized that they also needed to try new teaching methods. Marilyn Lund carried out proactive action research by herself in her own sixth grade class. Like Robert Hess, Marilyn focused primarily on her own professional development as an effective teacher. James Johnson engaged the students of his

eighth grade social studies class as partners in carrying out cooperative, proactive action research. James encouraged and helped his students to create new ways to improve the climate of the classroom.

Marilyn Lund*

Marilyn Lund graduated from college with a B.A. in sociology and two varsity letters in tennis when she was twenty-five. After two years of coaching adults in an athletic club, she decided to earn a master's degree in elementary education and a teacher's license. She was interested in the upper-elementary grades, believing that she was not effective with very young children. Now, as she turns thirty-one, she has completed her first year of teaching sixth grade at River Grove Elementary School.

All names of educators, schools, and communities have been changed.

Although her first year as a teacher was not a total failure (she will return to River Grove for a second year of probationary teaching), Marilyn wonders if perhaps she should have become a high school teacher. She feels frustrated with her principal because he did not help her understand eleven-year-olds better. She is also angry with herself for not doing a better job of starting the class last September. She remembers her wish to go fast and to put emphasis on homework and on academic excellence. Something went wrong right from the start.

Last May, the principal rated Marilyn as "adequate" on most scales during her evaluation but did rate her as "above average" in social studies and physical education. Those two subjects, after all, were her favorite to teach. The worst of it was that the principal rated her as "needs to improve" in classroom management, student rapport, and student discipline. She vividly recalls—even today, three months after the event—how strongly the principal pleaded with her to build more positive discipline into her classroom routines. "Marilyn," he said, "try to cut down on the negative with your students. Accentuate the positive. Play to their strengths." Now, after a summer of traveling, playing tennis, reading professional material about classroom group processes, and attending a three-day workshop on cooperative learning, Marilyn will start teaching twenty-eight sixth graders at River Grove in just a few weeks.

Marilyn's Solitary Dialogue

Marilyn's past self thinks: "I wasn't ready to be positive with and supportive of students last year. I was too concerned with my own security and self-esteem. I felt insecure, even scared, about working every day with eleven-year-olds. I didn't want to lose control of them, nor did I want to look incompetent to my colleagues or to the principal. I felt relieved when the principal didn't observe my class for the first ten weeks."

Marilyn's future self thinks: "I want very much to conduct my class differently this year. First, I want to heed my principal's advice to be more positive with the students. Also, I must worry less about myself and think more about how the students react to me. I plan to be much more observant of students' feelings this year. I want to accentuate the positive and to look for students' strengths."

Marilyn's past self thinks: "That's easy to think now, but when students don't follow my directions, I will become cross and make hurtful remarks to them just like last year. At times, last year, I flew off the handle and actualized my worst fears by really losing control. Talk about the self-fulfilling prophecy: Will this year be any different?"

Marilyn's future self thinks: "Yes, I will change because I truly want to become a more effective sixth grade teacher. After all, I have demonstrated my effectiveness many times teaching tennis to insecure adults. I also have demonstrated my effectiveness teaching sixth graders social studies and physical education. I can become a more caring teacher, because students' ideas and feelings are important to me. I know that I can become more receptive to students' ideas. I will listen more carefully than last year, strive to paraphrase students' ideas, and respect and show empathy for their feelings. I will use ideas I learned in the cooperative-learning workshop this summer."

Marilyn's past self thinks: "A year ago, I didn't reflect and plan like I am now. Last September, I hardly thought about the twenty-eight students and what they might be like as individuals. Last year, I primarily thought about the sixth grade curriculum, student achievement, and students following my directions. I wonder if I will be able to change those thought patterns."

Marilyn's future self thinks: "Yes, this year I will think much more about establishing trusting relationships with students. I will not seek domination or control. This year, instead of power over I will strive to establish power with the students. Above all, I will try to act warmer with students than I did last year. I shall try, also, to maintain a sense of humor and to laugh at my own mistakes. I want to be more open about my feelings and encourage students to share their feelings openly with me."

Marilyn's past self thinks: "That all sounds good, but like last year, I still think mostly about myself. Last year, I did not have strategies to teach students respect for one another. I am naive to think that changes in me alone will improve relationships in this year's class. Part of my problem last year was unfriendly relationships in the peer group. Lots of students felt rejected, neglected, or isolated from the most popular students in the class. The students' negative feelings did not only come from my actions; they were also communicated from student to student. How will I take peer-group influences into account this year?"

Marilyn's future self thinks: "This year during the first few weeks of school I plan to carry out a series of positive, get-acquainted, team-building activities that I learned this summer. I will relax more than last year. I will not push so hard the academic curriculum during the first few weeks of class. Also, I will appoint a committee of four to six students to help me monitor how the students feel about my teaching and about the peer-group climate. I will call that committee our sixth grade steering committee. I will tell the class a little about how quality circles function in business and how the steering committee will act like a quality circle. Membership on the steering committee will change every three weeks to give everyone a chance to participate during the first semester. I will also facilitate whole-class discussions to make group agreements on how we will work together in our class. I intend for all students to set the class rules."

Marilyn's past self thinks: "Those plans sound fine, but how will I know if they work? Last year, I did not realize how bad the students' feelings were until the principal observed the class in November. After he gave me feedback, I became defensive, wondering why he took so long to visit my class. I did not want to believe him. Also, by that time it was hard to modify the peer-group patterns that had formed."

Marilyn's future self thinks: "This year I will be more conscious of students' reactions than I was last year. Along with my daily observations of classroom interaction, which I will write about in

a journal, I will also regularly interview members of the steering committee about how the class is going. Furthermore, I will use a simple questionnaire with the students, perhaps after one month, to receive feedback from everyone about how 'I' and 'we' are doing. Now, I believe that I am ready to tackle the new academic year. I already feel good about this year, my second year of teaching."

Six-Step Proactive Process

Marilyn begins her second year of teaching with new vigor.

Step 1: Try a New Practice

Marilyn decides on three new get-acquainted practices for the first weeks of class:

- A human resource hunt in which she gives each student a list of experiences, attributes, and hobbies. The students hunt for classmates who have those "resources."

- Student biographies in which pairs of students interview each other about important life experiences. Each student writes a two-page biography of his or her partner. Over the next nine days of class, Marilyn asks the students to read the biographies to the class.

- A Tinkertoy construction in which groups of five students construct a symbolic representation of what they hope their classroom climate will be like in a few weeks.

During the second week, Marilyn establishes the first steering committee. She tells the committee her goal is for the students to help her in managing the class so they can all share in a supportive and healthy climate. She picks three girls and three boys with very different levels of academic ability for the first committee. She announces that all students will eventually serve as steering committee members. Marilyn works with the initial steering committee every day during lunch for one week, training its members to understand and use the task and social-emotional group roles. After the week of training, the steering committee meets with Marilyn twice a week to discuss problems, goals, and possible rules for classroom behavior and work.

After three weeks, Marilyn and the steering committee present their ideas about classroom rules and procedures to the class; they are discussed and voted on by everyone. Next, six new members are appointed to be the second steering committee. By the end of the first semester, the class—with the help of its steering committees—has created a list of classroom rules and procedures. As the year progresses, the steering committees help Marilyn solve discipline problems and keep the class focused on academic learning. The class decides to use the term *group agreements* instead of *rules*. (See Schmuck and Schmuck's *Group Processes in the Classroom* [1997] for more action ideas about starting a class.)

Step 2: Incorporate Hopes and Concerns

Marilyn's hopes are that the students will do the following:

- Get to know and appreciate one another

- Feel respect toward one another

- Value the different strengths and talents of one another

- Cooperate in sharing constructive leadership with her

- Solve interpersonal problems and resolve conflicts with one another

- Support one another in learning their academic subjects together

In contrast, Marilyn's concerns are that a few students will do the following:

- Act impolitely, perhaps aggressively, toward their peers

- Feel rejected, ignored, or isolated from their peers

- Refuse to follow group agreements, even when all students make the agreements

- Show a lack of focus on academic learning for sustained blocks of time

With this mix of ideal hopes and realistic concerns, Marilyn carries out the new classroom practices.

Step 3: Collect Data

Marilyn uses three methods to detect how the new practices affect the students.

First, she carefully observes students' reactions to the get-acquainted activities to make certain that every student's strengths and talents are publicly stated. She also watches herself and her use of positive statements as she strives to accentuate the positive. Every other day, Marilyn writes in a journal about her observations of the students and of herself. The reflective writing gives Marilyn opportunities to continue solitary dialogues about her professional values and practices throughout the year.

Second, Marilyn interviews members of the steering committee, one-on-one and as a group. She asks, "How do you think our class is going? Do you see any problems that we should try to solve? In what ways do you think our class could be improved? Are there changes you would like me to make? What ideas do you have to help all students learn more and better? What can we do as a class to help each of you learn math better, social studies better, language arts better, etc.?"

Third, Marilyn uses a questionnaire in mid-October to assess how "I" and "we" are doing. To obtain data about herself as a teacher, Marilyn uses a questionnaire, titled Our Teacher, in which she asks students to check one of the following scale points: much more, a little more, the same, a little less, or much less. The students rate Marilyn on the following behaviors: helps with work, yells at us, smiles and laughs, makes us behave, trusts us on our own, makes sure our work is done, asks us to decide, and makes us work hard. Figure 5.1 shows the Our Teacher questionnaire in its entirety.

To collect data about the class as a group, Marilyn uses a questionnaire, titled Clues about Classroom Life, in which she encourages students to act like detectives and write answers to the following open-ended questions: "What are some clues to a good day in this class? What things

Our Teacher

Pretend that I (your teacher) could change the ways I relate to you in school. For each number, check the box that best tells how you would like me to act in this class.

	Much more	A little more	The same	A little less	Much less
1. Help with work					
2. Yell at us					
3. Smile and laugh					
4. Make us behave					
5. Trust us on our own					
6. Make sure work is done					
7. Ask us to decide					
8. Make us work hard					

From *Group Processes in the Classroom* (Schmuck and Schmuck 1997, p. 168, Brown & Benchmark Publishers). Reprinted with permission from McGraw-Hill Companies.

Figure 5.1

happen that are signs of a good day? What are clues to a bad day in this class? What things happen that are clues that this class is not going the way it should or the way that you would like it to? What are some things that should happen a lot more than they do to make this class a better place for learning?" Figure 5.2 shows the Clues about Classroom Life questionnaire in its entirety.

Step 4: Check What the Data Mean

Marilyn uses four methods to check what the data mean.

First, she writes her reflections in a journal and rereads them from time to time. She reflects on the past, the present, and the future. Now and then, she reflects on whether she is reaching her aspirations and on how she is dealing with her expectations.

Second, Marilyn holds discussions once a week with the steering committee, where she presents some of the data she collects. She gives her own analysis and interpretation, then checks to see if the students agree or disagree with her findings. She encourages students to join her in the detection and judgment phases of the action research.

Third, Marilyn informally meets once every two weeks with a close friend who teaches fifth graders at another school in the same district. While the two eat dinner, they talk about what they do in their classes and reactions they get from their students. Afterward, Marilyn writes in her journal ideas and reactions she has received from her friend.

Fourth, Marilyn formally meets with the principal once a month to talk about how her class is going. She tells the principal about her new practices, invites him to observe, and describes the data she has collected. Together, Marilyn and the principal talk about how to keep students focused on academic learning while maintaining a positive classroom climate. The principal is pleased with Marilyn's personal creativity and professional maturity.

Step 5: Reflect on Alternative Ways to Behave

Marilyn uses the data feedback sessions with the students and the discussions with her friend and the principal to dream about alternative ways to teach. While she is pleased with the success of the new practices, Marilyn sees how they could be

Clues about Classroom Life

So that we may get some ideas about how to make life more interesting and important for everybody in this class, each of us needs to contribute ideas about what should be improved. What things happen that shouldn't happen? What ought to happen that does not? Imagine you are a detective looking for clues to a "good day" and a "bad day" in this class. Jot down what you might look for or might see to answer these questions.

What are some clues to a good day in this class? What things happen that are signs of a good day?

1. _____
2. _____
3. _____
4. _____

What are some clues to a bad day in this class? What things happen that are clues that this class is not going the way it should, or the way that you would like it to?

1. _____
2. _____
3. _____
4. _____

What are some things that should happen a lot more than they do to make this class a better place for learning?

1. _____
2. _____
3. _____
4. _____

From *Group Processes in the Classroom* (Schmuck and Schmuck 1997, p. 20, Brown & Benchmark Publishers). Reprinted with permission from McGraw-Hill Companies.

Figure 5.2

improved next time. For instance, although a few biographies were outstanding, many were too terse, some were poorly written, and a few were inaccurate. Some students asked fourteen or fifteen questions, while other students asked only two or three questions. Marilyn realizes that she should have done more to help students generate a standard list of interview questions and that the whole class should have created a standard outline for the biographies. Similar problems did not arise with the human resource hunt or the Tinkertoy construction because she prepared a standard list of twenty resources for the hunt and had each group of students work with the same number of Tinkertoys.

Upon reflection of the strengths and weaknesses of the steering committees, Marilyn decides she will start next year's first steering committee during the first week and spread out work on the biographies over the first three weeks. Also, Marilyn ponders whether she should form all steering committees right from the start so that every student knows he or she will get a chance to work closely with Marilyn to govern the class. Furthermore, those preformed steering committees could serve as basic support groups for cooperative-learning projects. Marilyn decides to discuss these ideas with her friend and her principal.

Step 6: Try Another New Practice

Marilyn decides to ask students to prepare another biography after the winter holiday. She forms students into groups of four. The task is for each small group to create a fictitious biography of a make-believe person who has six personal characteristics of each student member in the group. In other words, the fictitious character that each group creates will have a total of twenty-four characteristics—six actual qualities of each group member. Marilyn leads the whole class in discussions about the sorts of personal characteristics that might make up the biographies. Marilyn is pleased with the students' enthusiasm for the biography and looks forward to the results.

Marilyn is now fully involved in proactive action research and will continue the process throughout the year and beyond.

James Johnson*

After graduating with a B.A. in history and a secondary-teacher certificate, James went to work at Arlington High School. He taught world and American history to tenth and eleventh graders for ten years and served as an assistant coach for boys' football and a head coach of girls' track and field. Five years ago, James and the girls' track team took second place in the state track finals.

Changing demographics in the Arlington community showed that the number of tenth, eleventh, and twelfth graders was in decline while the number of elementary youngsters was increasing. The new demographics in Arlington called for K–5 elementary schools, 6–8 middle schools, and a 9–12 high school. The Arlington School District changed from a three-year to a four-year senior high school, creating two new middle schools to replace its one large junior high school. James and seven colleagues from the former high school were transferred to the middle schools. Although James did not want to leave the high school, he also did not wish to move from Arlington. So, he reluctantly agreed to teach eighth grade social studies at Jacobs Middle School. The results of his first year of middle school teaching were terrible. Now, he's a middle school teacher, no longer a coach, and frustrated with his job.

James decides to return to school in the summer to pursue a master's degree in school administration. He never thought about administration before, but in the face of his most frustrating year ever as a teacher, he decides administration might be a good idea for him. James feels that he could use the added salary and that his coaching experience has prepared him for management and leadership. He decides to get his feet wet before diving into graduate school and takes only two courses—educational leadership and alternative models of teaching.

James finds the two courses complement each other. Both give a good deal of attention to group work. In the educational leadership course, he is introduced to the skills of organization development, participatory management, and democratic leadership. In the course on alternative models of teaching, James learns about cooperative learning and cross-age tutoring. He writes a term paper about using cooperative learning in social studies, and he reads a few research reports on the benefits of older students tutoring younger students. He decides to try out some of these strategies in his own eighth grade social studies classes in the fall. He has found what he needs most—not new energy for school administration but new ideas to reinvigorate his teaching. He remembers why he loved coaching so much—the teamwork and the challenge of supporting one another in achieving excellence.

James's Solitary Dialogue

James's past self thinks: "In the past, to teach and to coach represented very different spheres of activity. When I taught, I lectured, asked specific questions about the text, drilled students for names and dates, assigned reading and workbook pages for homework, gave frequent tests, and assigned grades without giving students much constructive feedback. When I coached, I held discussions with the athletes, got to know them as individuals, sought to find out how they felt, encouraged them to do well, challenged them to improve, assigned groups of athletes to study their football plays or track relays together, and

---

All names of educators, schools, and communities have been changed.

sought ways to give constructive feedback, even in the face of defeat."

James's future self thinks: "In the future—in fact in just a month or so—I want to teach middle school students in the style of the coach I was, rather than the high school teacher I was. I want to use cooperative-learning techniques instead of lecture and drill, and I want to increase the students' engagement with learning. I want to encourage them to become teachers of one another and of younger students. Teaching is a good way to learn. I will use Aronson's (1978) Jigsaw Puzzle method and the Sharan's and Sharan's (1992) Group Investigation method. (Each of these methods is explained in Figure 5.3.) I will also find an elementary teacher who wants to collaborate with me on a cross-age tutoring project." (For original literature about cross-age tutoring, read Lippitt and Lohman [1965], and Lippitt, Eisman, and Lippitt [1969]).)

Six-Step Proactive Process

James Johnson conducts proactive action research, though not consciously as did Marilyn Lund. James's innovation also differs from Marilyn's in his decision to engage students as partners at every stage. James performs cooperative, proactive action research.

Step 1: Try a New Practice

On the first day of class, James tells the eighth graders about his reflections during the summer at the university. He describes how differently he acted as a teacher compared to how he acted as a coach. He tells the students he wants to act more like a facilitator and catalyst of their learning, rather than like a director and controller. He goes on to describe the three new practices he will use in this class:

- Aronson's (1978) Jigsaw Puzzle method, a cooperative-learning procedure to help everyone learn about the text and the workbook assignments.

- Sharan's and Sharan's (1992) Group Investigation method, another form of cooperative learning to help everyone apply social studies information to topics important to them.

Aronson's Jigsaw Puzzle

Aronson (1978) created the jigsaw cooperative-learning procedure to foster both interpersonal acceptance and student learning. Students teach one another portions of some curriculum content. They work in two sorts of small groups (e.g., learning teams and expert groups). Each learning team divides the curriculum content into equal portions so each member can teach a portion to the other members. Before the students in learning teams teach one another, those students in the class with the same portions of content to teach meet together in expert groups to review the content and to discuss how they will each teach it to their respective learning teams.

Sharan's and Sharan's Group Investigation

Sharan and Sharan (1992) created the Group Investigation method, which includes six steps:

1. A topic is specified and students are grouped into teams of six to do research on the topic.

2. The topic is divided into subtopics and each member selects a subtopic for individual study.

3. Individuals report back to their team on what they have learned. The team, in turn, integrates all contributions into a single outline and report.

4. The team reports to the whole class.

5. Team reports are evaluated by peers and modifications are made.

6. Teams turn their project reports in to the teacher for feedback and evaluation.

Figure 5.3

- Cross-age tutoring to help everyone learn how to help someone else to learn, which helps students learn about social responsibility and democratic citizenship.

Every Friday, James and the class will debrief how the "Johnson experiment" is proceeding. He will solicit feedback from the students about how helpful or unhelpful the three new practices are for their learning and development. He will make changes in classroom procedures according to the wishes of the majority, so long as what the majority wants is legal, moral, ethical, and acceptable to district policy. "We will study together," James tells the students, "ways to improve the climate of our class, so that every student has an opportunity to learn about social studies. We will learn about social studies through a study of our own social interaction."

Step 2: Incorporate Hopes and Concerns

James's hopes are the following:

- The students will become turned on to social studies
- He will feel renewed and reinvigorated in his teaching
- The students will master the eighth grade social studies curriculum
- Students will learn to apply social science to topics of importance to them
- The students will value helping one another learn

James's concerns are the following:

- Quite a few students will not carry their load in cooperative learning
- He might not have courage to stay the course if some students do not behave
- Some students will not strive to apply social science to important topics
- A few students might not relate well to younger students

Even with those concerns in mind, James remains enthusiastic about the new practices he has chosen to initiate.

Step 3: Collect Data

Since James is engaging students as partners in change, this third step is at the heart of his effort. Every Friday, for fifty minutes, James and the students study the three new practices together. James's primary research method is the focus-group interview, during which he raises questions about the new practices. For example, while the class uses Aronson's Jigsaw Puzzle method to learn contents of the text, James asks, "What do you see in Aronson's Jigsaw Puzzle method that helps you learn the contents of the text? What is it about Aronson's Jigsaw Puzzle method that does not help you learn the contents of the text? What are changes we might make in Aronson's Jigsaw Puzzle method to enhance your learning of the contents of the text? Please brainstorm out loud about any other thoughts or feelings you have about Aronson's Jigsaw Puzzle method." Instead of acting as sole interviewer, James often divides the students into pairs or trios so students can interview one another about Aronson's Jigsaw Puzzle method.

Prior to his initiation of Sharan's and Sharan's Group Investigation method, James takes a few Friday sessions to ask students to identify social issues and societal problems that are important to them. The content of these issues could be about the social effects of viewing television; whether aggression and hostility on the television or in the movies increases the viewer's aggressiveness; how relations are portrayed between races, ethnic groups, or sexes; how computers affect our lives; how aspects of the environment affect people's feelings; etc. Once the class generates a list of topics, James asks the students to choose two topics that interest them. Next, James creates small groups of students with similar interests. At this time, Sharan's and Sharan's Group Investigation method formally begins.

During the four weeks of Sharan's and Sharan's Group Investigation method, James uses Friday debriefing time to ask students how the investigations are unfolding and how the project groups might be improved.

Before implementing cross-age tutoring, James and the students spend several Fridays discussing how to be an effective tutor. Also, because the eighth graders are tutoring Sara Everton's second graders, James initiates discussions about seven-year-olds and what they are like. After the tutoring is underway, the Friday sessions focus on the challenges of effective tutoring and, in particular, on how to tutor second graders who misbehave or seem out of control.

In contrast to Marilyn, who uses multiple methods to collect data, James collects most of his data with group interviews. James and his students also use the method of unstructured observation, since all of them are participant observers. Although it might appear that Marilyn's mix of methods has more ingredients, the power of "consensual community" is actualized during James's Friday debriefings. By pooling the observations of all participants, James probably obtains valid data, particularly if he engages every student in the Friday meetings and does not make hasty judgments based on the ideas and perceptions of a few high-talking students. James increases the validity of his data if he is careful to encourage everyone to speak openly and honestly. He can facilitate full participation by calling on every student for a verbal contribution.

Step 4: Check What the Data Mean

James uses three methods to check the meaning of the data he and the students generate on Fridays.

First, he reflects on how the data match the concepts of group development, which he learned in his two summer graduate courses. He checks, in particular, whether students are appreciating one another's learning styles, sharing leadership functions, supporting one another to learn about social studies, and making constructive contributions to improve the new practices.

Second, James checks his data interpretations with the students' perceptions of the data. He presents the students' summaries of data he has analyzed and asks them about the accuracy or inaccuracy of his conclusions. He tries to focus these discussions on the here and now and probes students for their interpretations of what is

currently happening in the class. He follows up with questions about how to improve the three new practices next week.

Third, James meets once a month with Sara Everton. James brings data about cross-age tutoring from his Friday debriefings, and Sara brings her observations of how the tutoring is affecting her second graders. Together, James and Sara think about how to improve the tutoring program.

Step 5: Reflect on Alternative Ways to Behave

From his discussions with the students and with Sara Everton, James generates ideas about how to improve the three practices.

James decides that smaller expert groups work better when using Aronson's Jigsaw Puzzle method. He decides to try expert groups of two or three instead of five. He also decides to ask each student-expert to prepare a written summary of his or her part of the text prior to the expert-group discussion. The first change increases "air time" for each student in the expert groups. The second change increases students' individual accountability for studying the text before the expert-group meetings.

For Sharan's and Sharan's Group Investigation method, James decides to reduce the size of the project groups from six to four members to increase "air time" and involvement of each group member.

For cross-age tutoring, James believes the eighth graders should receive more training before becoming a tutor. He thinks, too, that the new training should include role-plays and discussion of typical tutoring problems.

Step 6: Try Another New Practice

At the start of the second semester, James's class moves to the computer lab and a group of eighth graders that had been in computer lab in the fall moves into social studies with James. James decides to revise the three practices right away with this new class.

Along with the modifications he thought about in step 5, James decides to try another new idea in cross-age tutoring. At a Friday debriefing, after his class completed two tutoring sessions with the second graders, James introduces a procedure he calls helping trios. He divides the class into groups of three and tells students each trio has three roles: tutor, helper, and observer. The tutor asks for help in becoming an effective tutor. The helper aids the tutor in figuring out how to become more effective. James instructs the helpers in a problem-solving method. The observer reflects out loud on how the helper was or wasn't helpful to the tutor. The roles within the trios rotate so that each individual member performs all three roles a few times.

James likes the helping trios because they portray "tutoring about tutoring," and they help the students view tutoring from three points of view. James feels renewed as a teacher and looks forward to the rest of the year.

Six Steps of Proactive Action Research

The steps of proactive action research are interdependent, circular, and continuous. The first two steps of initiation call for creativity, imagination, and risk taking. Steps 3 and 4 focus on detection. Data are collected to gauge merit and worth of the new practices. Steps 5 and 6 entail judgments about what went well and what should change. In the style of circular and continuous problem solving, step 6 is synonymous with step 1, and the action research spirals continuously. Figure 5.4 illustrates the connection between the six steps of proactive action research and the three phases of action research.

In proactive action research, creative problem solving and innovative practice precede data collection; however, the desire to risk doing something new often stems from one's previous unconscious data collections. These unconscious thoughts and feelings take the form of nagging frustrations, unfulfilled dreams, and unexpressed wishes. They are the psychological foundations from which one's search for new and better

practice emanates. They are the personal roots of proactive action research.

Step 1: Try a New Practice

Reflect on practices you want to initiate before trying them. Like Marilyn Lund, you might have a solitary dialogue between your past and future selves. Or, like James Johnson, you might reflect in a solitary dialogue about how you want to act anew with your students. Think about your values, your unfulfilled dreams, and the sort of role model you want to be. Now, try the new practice.

The term *new practice* applies differently from one educator to another. A new practice to one teacher is an old practice to another, forsaken by another, and unrecognizable or out-of-sight to yet another.

Robert Hess's writer's workshop strategy (see chapter 2) was new to him; although, hundreds of high school English teachers already use a form of it. Probably thousands of others do not know what it is, and perhaps a handful of others have tried and forsaken it.

Naturally, a host of classroom practices are new to Marilyn, who has taught for only a short time. Nevertheless, her idea to use the get-acquainted activities that she learned in a workshop is out-of-sight and out-of-mind to thousands of elementary teachers.

James's use of cooperative learning was new to him; although, hundreds of middle school teachers have used cooperative-learning methods for over a decade. It is likely that the majority of middle school teachers, however, do not know about Aronson's Jigsaw Puzzle method or Sharan's and Sharan's Group Investigation method—practices that Johnson learned at summer school.

The writer's workshop, the get-acquainted activities, and the cooperative-learning techniques include within them a very large number of concrete teacher practices. These practices are uniquely adapted into each teacher's repertoire. Thus, each teacher's version of an innovative practice is special and uniquely distinguishable from every other teacher's rendition of the same practice.

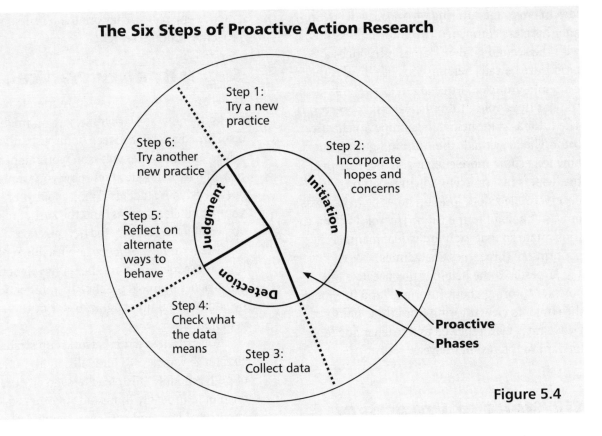

The Six Steps of Proactive Action Research

Step 1:
Try a new practice

Step 6:
Try another new practice

Step 2:
Incorporate hopes and concerns

Step 5:
Reflect on alternate ways to behave

Judgment

Initiation

Detection

Step 4:
Check what the data means

Step 3:
Collect data

Proactive Phases

Figure 5.4

Step 2: Incorporate Hopes and Concerns

Each new practice should be instrumental in moving you and your class from the current situation to a preferred state in the future. Try to be explicit about your goals for the new practice and be realistic about obstacles.

When writing about hopes in a journal, use such verb constructions as to achieve, to establish, to create, to facilitate, to foster, to lead to, and to produce. When writing about concerns, use such verb constructions as will accept, will be, will feel, will move away, will move toward, will reject, and will not want. Although concerns might be supportive, neutral, or unsupportive in relation to hopes, give special attention to concerns about events that may prevent the hopes from being reached.

Step 3: Collect Data

The research begins now, at least in the sense of collecting formal data. You can use question-naires, interviews, observations, or documents. The hopes and concerns generated in step 2 determine the content of the data collections. The data help assess whether progress is being made toward the desired goals and whether anticipated pitfalls are being avoided.

Because your effort to try new practices is unique, create your own data-collection instruments. James did that when he thought of the open-ended questions he used in the Friday debriefings. Ask about and observe your hopes and concerns. You are a better judge of the questions to use than a university-based researcher or an author of a traditional book on social-science methods. Still, others' research instruments can be put to use. Marilyn adapted others' questionnaire ideas to create the questionnaires Our Teacher and Clues about Classroom Life. The point is to use data-collection techniques that enhance your own professional maturity and the growth and development of your students.

Step 4: Check What the Data Mean

Raw data are merely numbers and words. They become useful when integrated into reflections on the past, present, and future. They take on meaning when they help answer questions about the merit and worth of new practices. Although fresh personal insight can be gained by silently reflecting on the data, group discussions about the data also help. Remember G. H. Mead's idea about the integral association between thinking and social interaction? (See chapter 1.) The data of action research become most useful when incorporated into conversations about teaching practices and the classroom with important others.

Perhaps the most important audience for conversations about the data is the classroom group itself. As James demonstrated, partnering with students offers a good way to check what the data mean. In James's classes, students not only learned about social studies through cooperative group work, but they also learned about social studies by doing a scientific study of James's social experiment. They experienced social science by doing action research on their social studies curriculum.

Other appropriate partners to interact with about the meaning of the data include

- A teacher-friend outside your school
- A trusted colleague within your school

- Parents of students
- A small team of colleagues in your school
- A principal

Step 5: Reflect on Alternative Ways to Behave

Think of the meanings gleaned from the data in step 4. What conclusions were drawn from conversations about the data? Are there some consistent themes that cut across those conversations? Now think of the day-to-day reflections on how the new practices unfolded. No information from others can substitute for your own reflection on the present about how the students are reacting. This is one reason why writing in a journal often and regularly can be helpful. The combination of others' understandings of the data and your own interpretations of what happened determine alternative ways to behave in the future.

Step 6: Try Another New Practice

You have now returned to the beginning. Either implement new practices with your current students or look for a fresh start with new student groups. Either way, one cycle of proactive action research has been completed. And, action research has been combined with reflective practice and constructive, sensitive problem solving.

You and Marilyn

Compare yourself to Marilyn Lund.

1. Describe similarities between Marilyn's situation and experiences you've had in your career as an educator.

2. Justify what you agree with in Marilyn's decisions.

3. Make a supportive argument for what you disagree with in Marilyn's decisions.

4. Apply any of Marilyn's strategies to your own work as an educator.

You and James

Compare yourself to James Johnson.

1. Describe similarities between James's situation and experiences you've had in your career as an educator.

2. Justify what you agree with in James's decisions.

3. Make a supportive argument for what you disagree with in James's decisions.

4. Apply any of James's strategies to your own work as an educator.

Step 1: Try a New Practice

Decide what new practices capture your imagination and inspire you to innovate. Brainstorm and list new practices to try next week, next month, or next year. Be specific and concrete. Be creative and take a risk.

Step 2: Incorporate Hopes and Concerns

For each new practice, write at least three hopes and three concerns. Try to be specific and concrete. Paint a mental picture of the class in which the new practice will be initiated. Be both idealistic and realistic. A solitary dialogue between your aspiring and reaching self and your concerned and cautious self might help.

New practice:

Hopes: Concerns:

Step 3: Collect Data

Jot down some possible data-collection methods you can use. What sort of a questionnaire would be appropriate? Should you carry out some interviews? What will you ask and to whom will you pose the questions? How about observing a few events? Should they be structured or unstructured observations? Are there any documents that might help you understand what is going on?

Step 4: Check What the Data Mean

Decide on who you should work with to analyze the data. Consider first and foremost the students. Can they play a role in helping you analyze the data? Perhaps you can invite the principal to help you, or perhaps you can recruit a colleague or two to collaborate with you. Sometimes, a few parent volunteers are appropriate. If you are part of a network of action researchers, obviously network colleagues could be asked to help. Write down some possible candidates and how they can help your analysis.

Step 5: Reflect on Alternative Ways to Behave

To start this reflection, brainstorm and list ideas to fine-tune the new practices. Then, try to think of a few radical changes. This stretches your creativeness. Next, sift through the ideas to find a few alternative ways to implement the new practices that are intuitively appealing. Then, take the ideas to a critical friend, students, a principal, or parents. How do others respond to these ideas? Finally, decide which modifications make sense. You should be the final judge of how to improve your own practice.

Step 6: Try Another New Practice

Consider the advice you have received. Think again about the data analyses from steps 3 and 4. Put those thoughts together with your step 5 reflections and decide on another new practice to try. Design an outline for this new practice with even more care than how you thought up the new practice in step 1.

Reflections

Reflect on chapter 5 by answering these questions:

1. In what ways would proactive action research be useful to you?

2. Can you create a few examples of new practices that you would like to try because of your reflections, reading, discussions with colleagues, or workshops you've attended?

3. Outline one or two new practices that you will try soon.

Chapter 6

Responsive Action Research

A good place to start toward classroom improvement is with facts about the interpersonal situation. A teacher's generalized concern for improvement can become a precise attack on a specific problem as information about the real state of affairs becomes available.

—Ronald Lippitt and Robert Fox

Teachers, supervisors, and administrators would make better decisions and engage in more effective practices, if they were able and willing to conduct research as a basis for these decisions and practices.

—Stephen Corey

I was introduced to action research as a doctoral student in social psychology at the University of Michigan. Ron Lippitt, my mentor and dissertation chair, demonstrated how action research works in his seminar The Dynamics of Planned Change. His view was that action research is responsive to data because data collection, referred to by Lippitt as diagnosis, necessarily precedes action.

At that time, teachers could not find much to read about action research, except for a few essays by Kurt Lewin (1948) and Ron Lippitt (1949) and *Action Research to Improve School Practices* by Stephen Corey (1953). All three authors conceived of action research as alternating cycles of diagnosis and action, with the initiation always being diagnosis. In the Lewinean tradition, it is assumed that effective "social engineers," whether attorneys, consultants, physicians, psychologists, or teachers, diagnose their clients'

problems and the dynamics of their situations before they act.

This model plays out in the experiences of Matt Reardon and Beverly Lee. Both teachers recognized a problem in their classroom, but they collected data from their students before implementing a new practice.

Matt Reardon*

Matt Reardon has taught English to lower-middle class students at Rosemont High School for three years. He loves to read serious classics, contemporary mysteries, short stories in *Field and Stream,* and essays in *The New Yorker.* He moves easily among William Faulkner, Amanda Cross, Barry Lopez, and Jane Smiley and alternates flexibly among novels, poetry, short stories, and expository essays. Matt also writes poetry, and he thinks earnestly of composing a novel about his

---

*All names of educators, schools, and communities have been changed.

eight years in the navy. Although Matt likes to teach, he would rather read or write. Matt teaches to live; he does not live to teach.

In the middle of November, Matt became frustrated with his twelfth grade English literature class. What is happening with this senior class has happened with other senior classes, but it has never been quite this bad. This class is made up of some of the brightest students at Rosemont, but many apparently do not read the assignments. Few students speak up in class when Matt questions them about the readings. He does not understand why these seventeen- and eighteen-year-olds do not seem to gravitate toward *King Lear*. After all, most have aging grandparents, and most, at least to some extent, have experienced the sibling rivalry of Cordelia, Gonerel, and Regan. Still, they come to class without a clue about the importance of this masterpiece. Instead, they watch the clock and count the minutes until lunch. They are hungry, Matt thinks, but only for food, not great drama, novels, and poetry.

Six-Step Responsive Process

Matt does not know how to engage his students. He finally decides to go directly to his students to find out what will help them become more interested in literature.

Step 1: Collect Data

Matt asks the twelfth graders to reflect silently about how his teaching does or does not help them learn English literature. He tells the students to print a plus sign on one side of a piece of blank paper and a minus sign on the other. He has them list the helpful things he does on the plus side and the unhelpful things he does on the minus side.

Next, Matt assigns each student to a boy-girl pair. He instructs the pairs to agree on at least two helpful things and two unhelpful things. With twenty-four students in the class, twelve pairs are formed. Matt asks each pair to meet with another pair and agree on three helpful things and three unhelpful things. He then brings two groups of four together to form groups of eight.

Those groups agree on at least four helpful things and four unhelpful things.

Matt tells the students in each eight-person group to count off from one to eight; he assigns person number five in each of the three groups to act as a spokesperson for his or her group. The three reporters come forward to the front of the room to form a panel. In pooling information from the three eight-person groups, the panel comes up with a total of eight helpful things and ten unhelpful things. (Figure 6.1 lists Matt's helpful and unhelpful teaching techniques.)

Matt thanks the students for their openness and honesty and tells them they will continue to work together with this information next week. When the bell rings and as the students file out for lunch, three students stop to tell Matt how much they appreciate today and his sincere effort to improve the class.

Step 2: Analyze the Data

Over the weekend, Matt looks at the data again and reflects on the themes he sees in them. He thinks that while the students appreciate his expertise in literature and find his information helpful, they also think he talks too much and does not facilitate discussion. In particular, Matt recognizes that his questioning style creates student anxiety and reluctance to speak. Matt wonders about the large number of assignments he gives and sees that superficial treatment might not be helpful to the students. Matt realizes that the very method he used to obtain these data could be used to get students more involved in discussions about the readings.

On Monday, Matt tells the students he wants to use the information they gave him to improve how the class operates. After he summarizes the themes of the data, Matt asks the students to return to their groups of four and brainstorm actions they would like to see him try.

Matt gives each four-person group a large sheet of blank poster paper with a magic marker. He tells each group to assign a recorder to print clearly the group's action ideas. After the recorders fasten their groups' reports to the wall, the students mill around the room to read what the

Rating Mr. Reardon's Teaching Techniques

Helpful

1. Gives information not in the text about authors
2. Explains characters well
3. Grades fairly
4. Shows enthusiasm for literature
5. Gives extensive feedback on papers
6. Has a good sense of humor
7. Does not favor one sex more than the other
8. Asks challenging questions

Unhelpful

1. Too much lecture
2. Covers too many authors
3. Assigns too much homework
4. Seldom asks us about how we feel or think
5. Drills us on what the authors' ideas are
6. Asks questions that make some of us afraid to make a mistake
7. Not enough time spent on difficult assignments (e.g., *King Lear*)
8. Not enough student-to-student discussion (today is the first time we held discussions in student groups)
9. Not always clear about what he wants in our papers
10. Sometimes uses words we do not understand

Figure 6.1

other five groups produced. Next, Matt tells each group to choose three action ideas that they like from the other groups. Matt announces he will study the action ideas and the students' preferences and give them feedback about the action ideas he will try.

Step 3: Distribute the Data and Announce Changes

The six groups produced a total of eighteen action ideas. The class chose six as their favorites. Matt writes those ideas on the chalkboard along with a few comments of his own in parentheses next to each. (See Figure 6.2.)

As Matt feeds the data back to the students and adds his reflections (information in the parentheses), he sees many students nodding approval. He asks them if he has understood how they want him to improve the class. Virtually all students chime in with a resounding, "Yes!" Matt announces the following action ideas to try for the next four weeks or until the winter holiday break:

We will reread *King Lear* and *Romeo and Juliet*. Each of you will reread both plays on your own, outside of class. Also, between now and the new calendar year, everyone will watch the videos of Jane Austen's *Pride and Prejudice* (the Lawrence Olivier production) and the more recent productions of *Persuasion, Sense and Sensibility,* and *Emma*. You will also be pleased to know that I want you to watch the video of Alicia Silverstein's *Clueless* because it is a kind of modern version of Jane Austen's *Emma*.

We will work on *King Lear* and *Romeo and Juliet* in small groups. I will assign you to work with different people on each play. We'll start with *King Lear* in groups of four. Tonight, everyone should quickly review the play. I know that it is a long play, but since we have recently studied it, a

Six Action Ideas to Improve Mr. Reardon's Class

1. Spend more class time in student groups to learn about the readings. (Use groups of two, four, six, or eight to work on English literature in ways parallel to how we have worked together during the past few days of class.)

2. Students come up with questions to ask Mr. Reardon about authors, their ideas, and literary themes. (Students initiate questions about literature that are important to them, in contrast to me drilling them about the readings. My question to the students: Will you read the assignments if we do that?)

3. Focus on just a few authors; spend more time on each. (Action ideas 4 and 5 below seem to follow from this idea.)

4. Reread *King Lear* and revisit *Romeo and Juliet*, which we read a while ago, but our

study of it was superficial. (Students want to recognize the importance of Shakespeare to English literature, want to understand his plays better, want to relate them to their lives, and a few of them recently found out that Leonard Bernstein's *West Side Story* is patterned after *Romeo and Juliet*.)

5. Read more of Jane Austen's books. (Since Hollywood discovered Jane Austen, students would like to know more about her and her novels.)

6. Students work together to report on readings to one another and to Mr. Reardon. (This action idea is an extension of idea 1 in this list; it could be integrated with ideas 2–5 if groups of students were to interview Mr. Reardon, for example, about Shakespeare and Jane Austen.)

Figure 6.2

quick rereading should be sufficient to get us started.

Matt then numbers off the four-person groups from one to six. He goes on to say:

Beginning tomorrow, groups one through five will become experts in the acts of the same number of their group. They will prepare reports on the key events and important lines of their group's act. Thus, group one will cover Act 1, group two Act 2, and so forth. Group six will have tomorrow to develop questions so that its members can interview me the next day about *King Lear* and Shakespeare. On this coming Friday, we will discuss how the small groups are working and try to make improvements so that everyone feels good about what he or she is doing.

On Monday, we will start with the reports of groups one and two on Acts 1 and 2. I will require each group to report to the whole class, with every member involved in the presentation. We will proceed with Acts 3 and 4 on

Tuesday and Act 5 and group six's report on the interview on Wednesday. Then, we will see where we are with *King Lear* before going on to *Romeo and Juliet*. By the way, how many of you were in that production of *West Side Story* we did here last spring at Rosemont? (Six students raise their hands.)

Step 4: Try a New Practice

Matt carries out the rereading of *King Lear* as planned. He is pleased with how involved most students are with the group work and in making reports to the whole class. Matt notes that those students who have not spoken up in class are now speaking in the small groups and to the whole class. He is impressed with the quality of the group reports and thinks that the interviewers did an adequate job.

For the study of *Romeo and Juliet*, Matt assigns some students to six groups of three each, and the rest to one group of six. The group of six comprises students who were in last spring's production of *West Side Story;* Matt has those students report on the similarities and differences between the two plays. Five of the other six groups report on the five acts of *Romeo and Juliet,* while the sixth group reports on an interview with Matt.

After the winter vacation, Matt continues the small-group methods with Jane Austen's novels. He assigns four groups of five each to work on one of Austin's four novels and assigns the fifth group to report on ways in which *Emma* shows up in the movie *Clueless.*

Step 5: Check Others' Reactions

Matt uses three methods to collect data on the students' reactions to the new practices. First, he observes participation and active involvement in the small groups and in the whole-class presentations. In particular, Matt is alert to students whose participation is relatively low compared to the others. He gives those students extra encouragement. Matt moves from group to group during small-group work to observe and encourage or to answer questions about the reading.

Second, Matt uses part of every Friday's class to interview students about the new practices. Matt often divides the class into groups of two or three so that all have an opportunity to speak. Matt sometimes combines groups to engage the students into a whole-group discussion. As a result of these debriefings, Matt is able to fine-tune small-group work as it progresses.

Third, Matt asks a colleague, Bob Harsted, to join the class as it reports about *Romeo and Juliet.* Bob teaches music, and he directed Rosemont's production of *West Side Story.* As the presentations proceed, Bob gives feedback to Matt and to the class about what he observes. The six-person group that was part of the *West Side Story* production invites Bob to participate in its presentation to the class. After class, Matt and Bob chat about ways to get students excited about literature, theater, and music.

Step 6: Collect Data

The following spring, Matt converts the list of helpful and unhelpful teaching techniques into a structured questionnaire. (See Figure 6.3 for the questionnaire.)

With this questionnaire, Matt assesses the merit of his new practices. He sees if students agree that he has continued the helpful techniques and discontinued the unhelpful techniques. To assess the worth of his practices, Matt develops an essay exam similar to ones he has used before and judges how well this class of twelfth graders compares to others. The data show significant improvement in students' feelings about the class and in what they are learning, but there are still a few problems. With these results, he feels ready to announce a few new action ideas that he will try for the rest of the academic year. Matt decides to make responsive action research an integral part of his teaching.

Beverly Lee*

After her freshman year in college, Beverly married and lived around the world because of her husband's position in the air force. While they were stationed in England, Beverly attended group-relations conferences at the Tavistock Institute of Human Relations. There she learned about Jacob Moreno's (1953) ideas about the power of the peer group in child development. At age thirty-nine, Beverly began work on a B.A. in elementary education and a teaching certificate. After graduation, Beverly was unable to obtain a regular teaching position, so she became a substitute teacher for two years and worked in six districts. She substituted mostly in elementary schools with upper middle-class families. Last August, Beverly got a job teaching fourth graders at McQueen Elementary School. McQueen is a K–5 school, serving a racially and ethnically diverse population of blue-collar and unemployed families.

After her first month of teaching, Beverly is surprised by a number of things about her twenty-seven fourth graders at McQueen. She is pleasantly surprised to find

- All twenty-seven students can read at least at a second grade level

---

All names of educators, schools, and communities have been changed.

Perceptions of How Our Class Operates

Below is a list of eighteen things that could happen in our class. Please circle one answer next to each item to show whether you strongly agree, agree, feel neutral, disagree, or strongly disagree (SA, A, N, D, SD).

In this class, Mr. Reardon

1. Gives information not in the text about authors
   SA   A   N   D   SD

2. Lectures too much
   SA   A   N   D   SD

3. Explains characters well
   SA   A   N   D   SD

4. Covers too many authors
   SA   A   N   D   SD

5. Is fair in grading
   SA   A   N   D   SD

6. Assigns too much homework
   SA   A   N   D   SD

7. Shows enthusiasm for literature
   SA   A   N   D   SD

8. Seldom asks us about what we feel or think
   SA   A   N   D   SD

9. Gives extensive feedback on papers
   SA   A   N   D   SD

10. Drills us on what the authors are trying to get across
    SA   A   N   D   SD

11. Has a good sense of humor
    SA   A   N   D   SD

12. Questions us in ways that make us afraid to make a mistake
    SA   A   N   D   SD

13. Does not favor one sex more than the other
    SA   A   N   D   SD

14. Does not spend enough time on difficult assignments
    SA   A   N   D   SD

15. Asks challenging questions
    SA   A   N   D   SD

16. Does not have enough student-to-student discussion
    SA   A   N   D   SD

17. Is not clear about what he wants in our papers
    SA   A   N   D   SD

18. Uses words we do not understand
    SA   A   N   D   SD

Figure 6.3

- The students are seldom absent or tardy

- Quite a number of parents have visited the school

- She relates well to all students regardless of their race, ethnicity, or sex

She is unpleasantly surprised by how rarely she sees the students of different races play or work together. The students of each racial group usually stick together. Although she has not seen intergroup bickering or fighting, Beverly observes that members of the different racial groups do not volunteer to work together on school work unless she requires them to do so. The few times Beverly required members of different racial groups to work together on a project, the students ended up working by themselves.

Six-Step Responsive Process

Beverly remembers what she learned at Tavistock and digs out college notes about how to measure social relationships in elementary classrooms. She finds a sociometric questionnaire titled How I Feel about Others in My Class. (See Figure 6.4 for the How I Feel About Others in My Class questionnaire.) She decides to give it a try.

Step 1: Collect Data

Beverly duplicates an alphabetical list of class members and numbers them from one to twenty-seven. She gives the class roster and a copy of the questionnaire to each student. Beverly asks the students to complete the questionnaire. She explains that she wants to establish a climate in

---

How I Feel about Others in My Class

Everybody has different feelings about everybody else. We like some people, we don't know others well, and we would like to get to know some people better. If the teacher knows the way you really feel about other members of your class, he or she can often plan things better. There are no right or wrong answers. (Use the class list to answer the following questions.)

1. Which three students in this class do you feel most friendly toward?

    The three I like most are:

    Student's number

    _____
    _____
    _____

2. Which three students in this class do you know least well?

    Student's number

    _____
    _____
    _____

3. Which three students in this class would you like to know better?

    Student's number

    _____
    _____
    _____

From *Group Processes in the Classroom* (Schmuck and Schmuck 1997, p. 129, Brown & Benchmark Publishers). Reprinted with permission from McGraw-Hill Companies.

Figure 6.4

---

which everyone feels friendly toward everyone else and where students can give her ideas about how to make the class more cohesive.

Step 2: Analyze the Data

Beverly finds that students of each racial group select students from their own racial groups when answering the first question on the questionnaire. In every case, a boy and a girl emerge as sociometric stars (chosen frequently) in each racial group. Thus, she finds six students (three girls and three boys) who are well liked by about one-third of the students in the class. Beverly has lunch with those six students and asks them if they will help her analyze data from the questionnaire. Beverly tells the class about the six students who will help her work on the data and assures everyone that all students will get the opportunity to work with Beverly on this project.

When the six students meet with Beverly, she shows them a large matrix for the data analysis. On the left side of the matrix, she has a vertical list of numbers from one to twenty-seven. Across the top of the matrix, she prints the letters L, O, and B. The L stands for liking choices; O stands for know-least-well choices; and B stands for like-to-know-better choices.

Beverly asks two African-American students to fill out the L column, two European Americans to fill out the O column, and two Native Americans to fill out the B column. She cuts up the completed questionnaires into three parts and gives each pair the sections it needs to do its tallying. After the data are arrayed, Beverly asks the six students to form an all-girls' group and an all-boys' group to discuss the following:

1. Which students do our classmates know least well? What kinds of things do they have in common?

2. Which students do our classmates want to know better? What kinds of things do they have in common?

3. What students, including the six of you, are chosen as most liked? What kinds of things do you and they have in common?

4. What ideas do you have for how we can get to know everybody better in our class?

Several themes emerge from the discussions of the two student groups:

> First, the students we know least well are newest to the class, quiet or shy, and are more often boys than girls. Second, students we want to know better are in all of the racial groups, a little more outgoing and social compared to those in the least-well-known group, and more often girls than boys. Third, the most liked students are like us, outgoing and social, and from both sexes and different racial groups.

When Beverly probes for the discussion groups' action ideas, a fourth and fifth theme emerge. The students say, "We, who are liked by others, should work more with the least-well-known students, and the whole class should try to find things that we all have in common."

Step 3: Distribute the Data and Announce Changes

Beverly asks the six students to feed back the sociometric data to their classmates. First, each pair reports what it tallied in each of the three columns. Second, the group of girls and the group of boys each reports on the themes and the action ideas. The girls report on the first theme and the boys report on the second theme. Beverly tells the class about the third theme. Then, the girls report on the fourth theme: people in the L column working more with people in the O column. The boys report on the fifth theme: the whole class working to find things that all students have in common. Finally, Beverly announces four activities that she will start the following day:

- Learning about being a friend
- Making a class book about friends
- Finding commonalities and strengths
- Reading trios to increase understanding of one another

Step 4: Try a New Practice

The next day, Beverly tells the class members they will work together for forty-five minutes every day to develop friendliness among classmates. She announces that the first activity is to learn about what it means to be a friend. She starts this activity by pairing up the students with one group of three. Beverly forms the pairs as follows:

- Students of different racial groups
- Highly liked students with least-well-known students
- Students the class wants to know better with one another

Beverly asks each pair to think of two friendly behaviors and two unfriendly behaviors. Next, she asks the pairs to form into groups of four and the group of three to remain a group. She asks the groups to agree on three important friendly behaviors and three important unfriendly behaviors. Next, Beverly asks each four-person group and the three-person group to report to the whole class. Each individual reports on at least one important behavior from his or her small group. Beverly prints the ideas on large sheets of poster paper in front of the class. She leads the whole class in a discussion to generate lists of ten friendly behaviors and ten unfriendly behaviors. Later, Beverly prints the two lists neatly on large cardboard posters to display on the classroom walls.

A few days later, Beverly starts the second activity: a class book about friends. In the initial phase, racially heterogeneous groups of three come up with sayings about friendship. For example, one trio came up with, "You can be yourself with your friends." Another trio came up with "Friends are there when you need them." Next, each trio draws a picture to illustrate its saying. Beverly puts the sayings and illustrations into a class book. Later, Beverly forms students into racially heterogeneous groups of five (with two groups of six) to make lists of characteristics of their friends. She also prints those characteristics in the class book. Beverly then assigns racially heterogeneous pairs (with one group of three) to create a story about friends. She prints those stories in the class book as well. At an open house, students show their parents those parts of the class book they created.

Beverly carries out two more activities. For the first activity, students work in small, racially mixed groups to come up with commonalities in the class. They also brainstorm strengths of individual students. For the second activity, she brings racially mixed trios to the "reading corner," where they read with her. She works with the reading trios while other students read silently, do computer projects, or receive special tutoring from middle school students.

Step 5: Check Others' Reactions

Beverly uses three research methods to assess how effective the new practices are. First, she observes communication between members of the different racial groups. She watches during formal class sessions, informal moments between formal activities, and at recess, at lunch, and after school.

Second, Beverly eats lunch once a month with different groups of five or six. She thinks of these gatherings as focus-group interviews,

during which she asks students for their perceptions and feelings about cross-racial friendships in the class.

Third, Beverly invites middle school students, themselves racially diverse, to her classroom to interview them about how they view intergroup relations in her class. She also asks them for ideas for improving the situation.

Step 6: Collect Data

Beverly uses another sociometric method, the roster-and-rating questionnaire (Schmuck and Schmuck 1997), to assess progress toward the goal of a more friendly, supportive, and cohesive fourth grade class. (See Figure 6.5 for the How I Interact with My Classmates questionnaire.) She gives the students a list of all twenty-seven classmates, asking them to rate the degree to which they would like to work or play with each classmate. She provides a four-point scale.

Beverly also asks each student to write a two-page essay about five peers in the class they have developed a friendship with during the school year. The essay should include reasons the author believes his or her feelings have become more friendly toward those five peers.

Beverly wants to find out whether the progress she perceives is corroborated by the subjective responses of the students. She also wants to see whether the students' two-page essays help her form new insights into how friendships were formed in this class. This might

How I Interact with My Classmates

Please rate your twenty-seven classmates on the following activities:

1. Working together in a small group (circle one):

   Yes, for sure   Yes   Neutral   No

2. Playing games together outside the class (circle one):

   Yes, for sure   Yes   Neutral   No

3. Read together with the teacher (circle one):

   Yes, for sure   Yes   Neutral   No

4. Attending a class party together (circle one):

   Yes, for sure   Yes   Neutral   No

5. Writing together in class (circle one):

   Yes, for sure   Yes   Neutral   No

Figure 6.5

give her new ideas about how to integrate friendship formation into academic learning.

Beverly is pleased with the results. Many new friendships have formed and every student is now known well by others. She is especially pleased with the many cross-race friendships that have formed in the class and how well students cooperate with one another on academic learning.

Six Steps of Responsive Action Research

Slower to move to a new practice than its proactive counterpart, responsive research's first four steps constitute initiation. This phase incorporates four practices new to students:

1. Teachers ask students for ideas on improving the class

2. Teachers engage students as partners in data interpretation

3. Teachers feed back the students' data and their own interpretations of the data

4. Teachers announce new practices they intend to try

Although step 5 is detection and step 6 is judgment, both detection and judgment also occur as part of steps 1–4. Responsive action research, simply stated, entails diagnosis, action, and evaluation. Figure 6.6 illustrates the connection between the six steps of responsive action research and the three phases of action research.

Step 1: Collect Data

On the threshold of initiating responsive action research, you sense that your teaching could improve and a few classroom events could be designed differently. Although ambivalent about soliciting critical feedback from students, doing so permits more effectiveness in teaching. Collect objective data about students' thoughts and

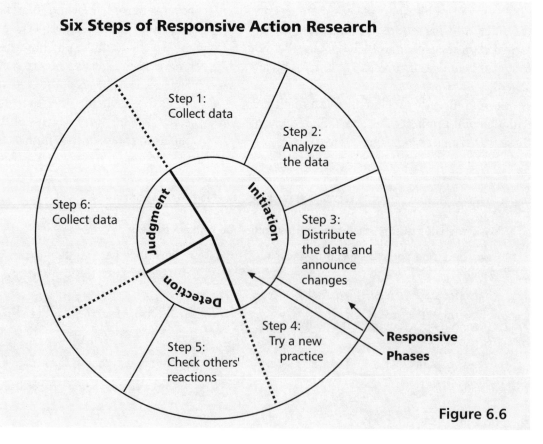

Six Steps of Responsive Action Research

Step 1: Collect data

Step 2: Analyze the data

Step 3: Distribute the data and announce changes

Step 4: Try a new practice

Step 5: Check others' reactions

Step 6: Collect data

Judgment

Detection

Initiation

Responsive Phases

Figure 6.6

feelings and initiate a constructive strategy to improve current classroom interaction patterns.

The initial data collection is short and simple. It can be as straightforward as the following examples:

- Matt Reardon's plus and minus signs on two sides of blank paper

- Pairs of students discussing strengths and weaknesses of teaching methods

- Students picking four peers to work on a project

- A simple sentence-completion inventory

- An open-ended "Who Am I?" questionnaire

- A sociometric questionnaire

- A colleague's observation

- Audiotaping a classroom discussion with students

Collect data from students in a public and official manner to communicate the importance of the endeavor. It is important to convey to everyone in the class that the data will be used to bring about improvement.

Step 2: Analyze the Data

Analyze the data to find recurrent themes and patterns. The analysis can be done alone, as Matt did, or with a small group of students, as Beverly did. A colleague, or the whole class, can also help analyze the data.

An important aspect of data analysis is finding ideas for action. While the themes or patterns depict how students think and feel about current classroom interactions, action ideas represent instrumental strategies for moving from the current situation to a more ideal place. The combination of themes and action ideas generates creative new practices. For example, Matt realized that students could question him instead of him questioning them. Beverly discovered the power of racially mixed student groups working together on a project.

Searching for themes and action ideas opens a window to the present and maps the future. Do not get preoccupied with whether the data are valid and reliable in the psychometric sense.

Internal validity rather than external validity is the main concern. If the themes and action ideas have the ring of truth to you, you are on the right track. Satisfy yourself that the data are helpful and that the new actions feel right.

Step 3: Distribute the Data and Announce Changes

Select a limited number of themes and action ideas. Do not attempt to cover all the data or all the possible actions that you could take. The key to this step is to show a logical connection between what you learn from the data and the changes you implement. State to the class what specific changes you will try during the next few weeks or months. This presents students with a road map of future classroom interaction, reasserts the seriousness and importance of the change effort, and offers a contract to which the teacher and the students are held accountable. However, the announcement should not cause a continuance of new practices that turn out poorly. For that reason, the announcement should foreshadow steps 5 and 6.

Step 4: Try a New Practice

Implement practices that are new to you and to the students. Give the new practice at least two months to take shape and have an effect. Do not invite colleagues or the principal to observe the innovation too soon, unless they were collaborating with you from the start. Allow several success experiences before formal evaluations. Fine-tune along the way and make needed modifications as challenges arise. Reflect on the present, but stay the course.

Step 5: Check Others' Reactions

While you are implementing the new practice, remain vigilant to yourself and to your students' reactions. This is the time to reflect on the present. Remain sensitive to the present flow of classroom interaction, to expressions of feelings, to approach and avoidance behaviors, and to ways the class does or does not cooperate as a group.

Check on how others react through unstructured observation. Watch specifically for smiles and laughter, for heads shaking in agreement, for eye-to-eye connections, for heads bent toward one another, and for the ease with which students approach you and one another. Try structured observation by counting rates of talking; by listening for paraphrasing, summarizing, and feeling statements; and by tuning in to the frequency of statements that use words such as we, us, our group, and our class.

Interview students about their perceptions and feelings. Matt did this when he interviewed students about their group work in English literature during his Friday debriefings. Beverly did it when she interviewed six different students at a time and invited the middle school students to her classroom. Think about how to interview individual students, small student groups, and the whole class about their reactions to the new practices.

Step 6: Collect Data

After the new practice has been tried, there are three reasons to collect data:

1. To assess whether the new practice has merit (Are the students satisfied with the practice? Have they developed more positive attitudes? Do they show more appreciation for one another and for the curriculum?)

2. To judge whether the new practice has worth (Are the students learning the curriculum as hoped? Do they behave differently toward one another and toward you? Do the students perform better on academic tasks? Are there things they can do now that they can take with them next year?)

3. To uncover new themes or action ideas that emerged while the new practice was implemented (Are there any unexpected gains from the new practices? Are there any unintended negative consequences from the practice?)

Now, look for a new focus for the next cycle of action research. You are fully engaged in continuous improvement.

You and Matt

Compare yourself to Matt Reardon.

1. Describe similarities between Matt's situation and experiences you've had in your career as an educator.

2. Justify what you agree with in Matt's decisions.

3. Make a supportive argument for what you disagree with in Matt's decisions.

4. Apply any of Matt's strategies to your own work as an educator.

You and Beverly

Compare yourself to Beverly Lee.

1. Describe similarities between Beverly's situation and experiences you've had in your career as an educator.

2. Justify what you agree with in Beverly's decisions.

3. Make a supportive argument for what you disagree with in Beverly's decisions.

4. Apply any of Beverly's strategies to your own work as an educator.

Step 1: Collect Data

List some data-collection methods you can initiate. Do you want to do a needs assessment? Is there a questionnaire that could get you started? How about some interviews to give you rich data about what's happening? Perhaps you should design a few strategic observations. Are there documents that could help you understand what is going on?

Step 2: Analyze the Data

Think of a creative way to analyze the data and list some people who might assist with the analysis. Seek to engage students in tallying and organizing the data. Further, try to convene a discussion with students about what the data mean. Are there colleagues who will help you understand the data? Or, perhaps the principal or assistant principal might collaborate with you in the analysis. Maybe a community volunteer or a few parents might help. Whatever you do, initiate collaboration with others to make the analysis of data more valid.

Step 3: Distribute the Data and Announce Changes

Brainstorm the various audiences for whom you can distribute the data. Students will often be the primary audience for data feedback, but you should also think about key colleagues, other teacher leaders, the principal, and the entire staff. Decide on the best sequence of feedback sessions with the various audiences. Also, strive to create logical connections between the data and the changes you want to try.

Step 4: Try a New Practice

Outline the new practice before start up. What special materials, such as worksheets, transparencies, slides, etc., will you need? How will you want the students seated? Create a rough timeline and do your best to stick with it, but don't become a slave to the clock. During the first few days of the new practice you will fine-tune as you go. Concentrate on reflecting on the present.

Step 5: Check Others' Reactions

Base your fine-tuning of the new practice on your own perceptions of how the students are reacting. Also, move outside yourself and beyond your subjective observation by interviewing students about their views on what is happening. Take some time and reflect on how the new practice is working and list some possible interview questions to ask your students.

Step 6: Collect Data

Reflect on the past on the data-collection methods that worked best in step 1. Repeat those. Be creative and list new items to your best methods that will help you assess students' reactions to the new practice of step 4. To judge whether the new practice has increased student learning, use questionnaires, interviews, or observations to create tests. Write down which methods will work with your students and why.

Reflections

Reflect on chapter 6 by answering these questions:

1. In what ways would responsive action research be useful to you?

2. Can you create a few examples of questionnaires, interviews, observations, and documents that you would like to try?

3. Can you outline one or two specific research methods that you will try soon to launch responsive action research?

Chapter 7

Processes of Cooperative Action Research

*Teachers cannot create and sustain the conditions for the productive
development of children if those conditions do not exist for teachers.*
                                                                    —*Seymour Sarason*

*Action research . . . is noncompetitive and nonexploitative and enhances
the lives of all participants. This collaborative approach to inquiry seeks
to build positive working relationships.*   —*Ernest T. Stringer*

In *The Predictable Failure of Educational Reform,* renowned psychologist Seymour Sarason (1990) reminds school administrators and educational policymakers that teachers engage in change and development as much as their students. Teachers assume the role of responsible adults in the school, but this does not mean they are not growing human beings. Sarason argues that teachers need nurturance and reinforcement to support their professional development, just as students need nurturance and reinforcement to engage in academic learning.

Australian educator Ernest Stringer helped workers perform community-based action research in a variety of community and organizational settings. Stringer's community-based action research is analogous to cooperative action research in schools, in which teachers work together to reach goals that are important to all of them. Stringer argued that community-based action research is successful when participants work together with honesty, nondefensiveness,

openness, and a spirit of cooperation and equality (Stringer 1996).

Cooperative school-based action research establishes positive working relationships among administrators, teachers, specialists, classified staff members, parents, board members, and students. Along with the skills of reflective practice, the knowledge of research methods, and an understanding of the steps of proactive or responsive action research, cooperative action research requires the skills of group dynamics.

School participants with common concerns and interests use cooperative action research to reflect on and inquire about educational issues. The word cooperative refers to joint efforts to reach the same end, while the word collaborative refers to joint efforts to promote individual ends. Thus, examples of action research in chapter 8 are cooperative, while most instances of mutual effort portrayed in chapters 5 and 6 are collaborative. Three social-psychological processes characterize effective cooperative action research: positive social support, critical friendship, and probing conversation.

Positive Social Support

Positive social support requires team members to communicate esteem, respect, and mutual obligation to one another. Figure 7.1 lists some important Traits of a Supportive Community.

Positive social support enhances the ability of team members to feel secure and to perform competently. For instance, soldiers perform their duties more effectively when interpersonal relations in their platoons are friendly and supportive. Industrial work groups perform more successfully when interdependent workers communicate mutual respect for one another. Participants' ideas in problem-solving groups are accepted and used more when they are friendly with other group members. Students achieve better academically when they feel accepted and respected by their classmates (Schmuck and Schmuck 1997).

When people cooperate in groups, they frequently feel anxiety about how they will perform. They think: "Will I be competent here? Will I be able to contribute to this group's success? Who will appreciate me in this group? Will they think I am carrying my load? Will people listen to my ideas? How can I exert my will here?" These questions reveal human beings' deep concerns about competence, acceptance, and influence.

There are three big needs to be met in positive social support: achievement, affiliation, and power. Supportive communication within cohesive groups enhances the participants' self-esteem by satisfying their needs for achievement, affiliation, and power. The need for achievement is satisfied by joining together to solve important challenges. The need for affiliation is satisfied by expressing positive feelings, help, and obligation to one another. The need for power can be satisfied by acknowledging the importance of one another's ideas and feelings as they work together. Without a strong foundation of positive social support, cooperative action research will not succeed.

Critical Friendship

Constructive criticism exchanged between friends helps convert negative energy into positive energy and diffuses anxiety. Since teachers perform most of their daily routines without adult interaction, they need to learn and practice how to exchange constructive criticism and how to act as critical friends.

In one of my graduate seminars with highly seasoned administrators and teachers, I ask pairs of "critical friends" to exchange feedback about their essays on educational policy and research before turning them in. Using critical friendship as a device is helpful because virtually every experienced adult student feels insecure about his of her ability to write competent research papers, master's theses, and doctoral dissertations. Pairing these students helps them cope with their fear of failure in writing. (See Figure 7.2 for a list of Schmuck's Collaborative Peer-Tutoring Steps.)

Critical-friendship pairs work best when preceded by team-building exercises and cooperative-learning activities. Participants pick their partners and initially meet with the instructor for input,

---

Traits of a Supportive Community

Supportive communication includes

- Understanding others' ideas and feelings
- Acknowledging others' beliefs and values
- Showing concern for others' welfare and happiness

- Giving help and acknowledging obligation
- Expressing empathy and positive feelings

Figure 7.1

Schmuck's Collaborative Peer-Tutoring Steps

In the style of two-way, collaborative peer tutoring, participants work through the following steps with each other:

1. Each participant writes a 500-word draft about an educational issue he or she would like to research.

2. The partners exchange their drafts for an initial reading.

3. Without referring to the draft, each writer explains to his or her partner the main points to be made in the essay.

4. Each listener (tutor) gives feedback to the writer about gaps between the essay and the oral summary. This helps each writer see how his or her draft could be written more clearly.

5. The partners tell each other how they will rewrite their essays.

6. Each partner reads the other's draft, circling anything that is unclear, inaccurate, grammatically incorrect, etc. This helps each writer become more precise in his or her prose.

7. Each student spends time alone to rewrite the draft.

8. The partners either hand in the essay or exchange the second draft with their partner for additional constructive criticism.

Figure 7.2

guidance, and support. The pairs are encouraged to recognize their common ground and to understand the assumptions that undergird the critical friendship procedure (see Figure 7.3).

Critical friendships can enhance effectiveness of both individual and cooperative action research. An example of individuals working collaboratively is when Marilyn Lund (see chapter 5) and the fifth grade teacher from another school used critical friendship to critique each other's projects. Another example is when two teams of action researchers, each doing their own cooperative action research, use critical friendship to critique one another's projects. A single team also uses this process by periodically standing back

from business as usual to critique its own project. Positive social support and critical friendship work hand-in-hand to enhance the effectiveness of all kinds of action research, but they are essential to the success of cooperative action research.

Probing Conversation

Probing conversations occur between critical friends in one-on-one interviews or within or between teams in focus-group interviews. Like exchanges between critical friends, probing conversations entail mutual help and reciprocal obligation between egalitarian partners. These

Assumptions that Undergird the Critical Friendship Procedure

- Positive social support alone does not facilitate learning, development, or problem solving. Critical feedback about shortcomings must accompany positive social support, allowing the recipient to correct mistakes, reduce errors, and improve his of her understanding.

- People accept and use criticism more enthusiastically when it comes from an empathic peer rather than an impersonal source.

- Positive social support and constructive criticism facilitate learning when they are delivered within the social framework of an egalitarian and reciprocally helpful relationship.

Figure 7.3

conversations go beyond the usual content of interviews between critical friends by focusing on larger teaching and learning issues in the school.

Probing conversations among educators usually take place during faculty meetings, within grade-level teams, at departmental gatherings, during site-council or special task-force meetings, or at staff retreats and inservice workshops. Conversations between new partners typically last for about ninety minutes. Each individual or team has the opportunity to talk for forty-five minutes about significant educational issues that they believe can be affected by changing school practices.

During probing conversations, participants, whether individuals or groups, strive to mirror their partners' ideas and perceptions by frequently paraphrasing and summarizing their partners' statements. The interviewers support *and* confront the others' reflections by pushing for clarity and specificity. The conversation deepens each participant's concerns about effective teaching and learning.

Since probing conversations of this sort rarely occur among teachers in the same school—at least as formal events—have the collaborating or cooperating partners (individuals or teams) meet privately with each other. At the initial gathering, do not expect the pairs to report to others about their conversations. Later, after action research becomes a way of life in the school, probing conversations about teaching and learning will occur in public forums. At that time, individual administrators or teachers might present their action-research designs to site councils or special task forces, while teams might report on their cooperative plans to the whole staff. Indeed, public presentations enhance the power of action research in the school. The deep reflection, open conversation, and planning required to create a coherent public presentation serve as an impetus for team members to coalesce their ideas and give extra cooperative energy to their project. Making public presentations together also facilitates team cohesiveness. Figure 7.4 is an example of A Probing Conversation.

A Probing Conversation

After attending a conference on teacher research, four young teachers from the same middle school decide to work together on some sort of research project. They report this interest to their principal who says she will support their effort. The principal asks a seasoned teacher to take the role of facilitator and to engage the research team in a probing conversation.

FACILITATOR: Let's start with the four of you brainstorming issues in the school—particularly problems in teaching and learning—that you have been reflecting on lately.

TEACHERS:

- Students don't show respect toward our special-needs youngsters

- Our faculty is not very cohesive

- Our social studies curriculum is textbook dominated

- Too many students are lackadaisical about school work

- Our students have a love-hate relationship with the businesses in the area

- Middle school students are confused about who they are and where they are going

FACILITATOR: Tell me more about the problems.

TEACHERS: (The teachers elaborate.)

FACILITATOR: OK, good. I heard you refer to six different problems. Let me try to paraphrase each one. (The facilitator paraphrases the list of six). Am I accurate?

TEACHERS: Yes.

FACILITATOR: Now, talk about ways in which you think the six problems might be interrelated.

TEACHERS:

- Early adolescence

- Confused identities

- School doesn't really engage their interests

- Many of our colleagues are burned out trying to teach these kids

(continued on next page)

Figure 7.4

Focus-Group Inteview continued from page 102

- Teachers are trying to build a life away from the job to keep their sanity
- We expect students to sit and listen for too much time

FACILITATOR: Can you give me some examples?

TEACHERS: (The teachers give specific examples.)

FACILITATOR: Let me summarize what I think the problems are in teaching and learning that concern you the most: Kids of this age are active yet confused. They are difficult to work with in the traditional school culture. Teachers get worn out in trying to motivate the students; they prefer to stay away from the kids as much as possible. It strikes me that both the students and the teachers need activities or events to raise their spirits. Am I accurate?

TEACHERS:

- You are on to something; yes, the students and the teachers both seem to want to avoid each other
- I like your phrase "raise their spirits"; this is a school without much spirit
- Yes, we should try something new to cut through this lack of spirit
- Perhaps we could do something with school spirit or with our dull social studies curriculum

FACILITATOR: Now, let me see if I understand how you see the current situation. There is rather low morale all around with the students and the teachers. Students and teachers alike are lackadaisical about schoolwork. Correct?

TEACHERS: Right on!

FACILITATOR: And, let me see if I understand how you see the ideal targets you wish to strive toward. You want a school culture in which everyone is enthusiastic about teaching and learning together. Am I accurate?

TEACHERS: Yes, indeed you are.

FACILITATOR: OK, let's brainstorm the helping and hindering forces you see in the situation. What is helping you move toward your target?

TEACHERS:

- A supportive principal
- A modern facility

- Supportive parents
- Some area businesses support our students
- A few teachers who will try something innovative
- Some students who are enthusiastic about the school

FACILITATOR: What is keeping you from moving toward your target?

TEACHERS:

- Many worn out veteran teachers
- The development stage of students
- Textbook dominated curriculum
- Outdated faculty philosophy on proper teaching
- Some businesses reject our students' presence

FACILITATOR: Now, let us brainstorm together about new actions you might take to reduce the hindering forces and increase the helping forces

TEACHERS:

- Throw out the text in social studies
- Organize small groups of students to cooperate in community service projects
- Get interested faculty to join us in a social studies program of community service projects

FACILITATOR: Let's brainstorm about research data you might collect to see how others in the school community relate to the problem.

TEACHERS:

- Questionnaire for students about the social studies curriculum
- Interview with our colleagues about ways to improve teacher and student morale
- Interview with business people in the area
- Library research on community service projects in middle schools
- Observations in a few social studies classes that get high ratings from the students

FACILITATOR: I hope I have helped you get a running start on your cooperative action-research project.

Effective Group Dynamics

Successful cooperative action research requires participants' competence in three domains: professional reflection, trustworthy research methods, and effective group dynamics.

Excellence in the first two does not compensate for deficiencies in the last. For cooperative action research to work well, it requires effective group dynamics.

Ten Tips for Group Dynamics

The following are ten tips about group dynamics to keep in mind.

Tip 1: Establish Feelings of Membership, Inclusion, and Trust

Participants must feel secure in their group membership. Secure membership means that each member of the action-research team feels confident that other members want him or her to be an integral group member. Spend time helping every member learn a few personal things about every other member. Feelings of inclusion pave the way for the development of interpersonal trust, whereby members feel secure in being themselves and do not feel threatened to disagree or hold different points of view.

Tip 2: Foster Shared Influence and Dispersed Leadership

All participants should believe they can affect what the group does. Shared influence means each member contributes some important content to the action-research design and that each individual's contributions dovetail with other members' contributions. Dispersed leadership similarly means that everyone rotates task and social-emotional roles in a reciprocating fashion to help the group carry out all six steps of action research.

Tip 3: Accentuate Friendliness and Cohesiveness

Although all members of an action-research team do not need to be friends, cooperation is

smoother if participants express friendly feelings toward one another. This is accomplished when members perform social-emotional roles during group work. Friendliness is enhanced when everyone values a few important things about everyone else and has insights and knowledge about every other member. Cohesiveness means that group members identify themselves as a team and that they pull together and support one another in carrying out the action research.

Tip 4: Cope with Social Status Differences

When action-research teams comprise teachers, administrators, classified staff members, students, parents, board members, or citizens at large, significant social-status differences among the members are inevitable. In such diverse groups, members whose status is lower than others often participate less and feel left out. Care must be taken to ensure that every member, regardless of status, is treated with the same attention and respect as every other member. The group should use sound meeting skills to see that every member's ideas and skills are used to plan and execute the action research.

Tip 5: Use Sound Meeting Skills

A convener and a recorder should facilitate team meetings. Conveners have authority to move the group through tasks, bring silent members into discussion, and remain vigilant in getting the group through its agenda. Recorders help conveners keep the group on task by writing down the important decisions made by the group and, from time to time, by summarizing decisions during the meeting. As the team matures, the roles of convener and recorder can be rotated through the membership. The following meeting skills are useful tools to keep the group focused on the action research:

- Use orienting statements to define the information, the target, the problem, or the specific task to be worked on. They provide opportunity for everyone to be clear about the present focus of the group's work.

- Set the agenda to make clear the tasks the team will work on during the meeting. Often high-priority work is focused on first, or at least early, to ensure that it will be accomplished while the energy of group members is high.

- Use summarizing statements to help the team's work accumulate. Often, the recorder prints important information on poster paper or a chalkboard so that everyone is clear about what is being accomplished.

- Make procedural statements to help teammates reflect on the processes of their discussions. They ask members whether they want to carry on with what they are doing now or if they want to change direction.

- Take a survey, going from individual to individual to see how each member stands on an issue or a potential decision. A survey is taken to get information about what the members think about a certain topic. It is not a time to debate or evaluate.

- Observe which members do not say much and attempt to bring silent members into the discussion. People who wish to speak but can't get into the flow of the group need help to contribute.

- Encourage the participation of quiet members, by actively supporting others to contribute.

Tip 6: Use Sound Communication Skills

Along with sound meeting skills, the work of a cooperative action-research team can be enhanced by using the following communication skills:

- Paraphrase, using one's own words to restate what another person has said. Paraphrasing allows one to see if the initiator understands the meaning behind another person's statement.

- Describe behaviors, stating either the overt behaviors of others or telling about one's own behaviors. Behavior description helps the group become focused and specific about educational issues, preferred targets, and understandings of the current situation.

- Describe feelings, pinpointing one's emotional state about an issue and putting it into clear language for others to understand. Describing feelings helps the group become focused and specific about the basic values that undergird the action research.

- Make clear statements, succinctly telling others about one's ideas using only three or four sentences. A clear statement can be accurately paraphrased by others.

Tip 7: Reach Understandings About Group Agreements

Early on, the action-research team should reach agreements about how it wants to function. The discussion could focus on each of the above tips. To form group agreements, each member should get a chance to state a practice that he or she would like to see the group adopt. The group discusses each proposal until it reaches agreement. The recorder prints the agreements on poster paper and later disseminates them on regular paper to everyone. From time to time, the convener reminds the group of its agreements.

Tip 8: Strive to Make Decisions by Consensus

Group consensus is a special kind of decision-making process that requires a thorough discussion and a spirit of cooperation. Consensus is different from a unanimous vote because it does not mean everyone agrees. Rather, group consensus means that enough group members are in favor to carry out a decision. Those who remain in doubt understand the group's decision and help with its implementation. Three steps are key to successful group consensus:

- All members understand the issue under consideration (assessed through paraphrases and a survey).

- All members voice their views, and the convener and the recorder prod the group to reach common ground, to negotiate, and to compromise.

- Those who doubt the decision try it for a prescribed period without sabotaging it (again a survey is also helpful here). As the action-research team grows in maturity, it uses consensus decision making naturally and routinely.

Tip 9: Take Time to Debrief the Team's Group Processes

Debriefing entails an examination of the group's interaction after a meeting. The convener and the recorder ask, "Are we living up to our group agreements? Are we using the meeting and communication skills? How might we improve our next meeting?" Debriefing is like a small action-research project in that the group collects data from itself to initiate new procedures to improve its functioning.

Tip 10: Look to See if There Is Group Follow Through

The team's efforts are only as good as the quality of its work between meetings. Most action-research teams periodically establish a division of labor as they proceed through the six steps. Subgroups form to prepare data collection methods, collect data, and analyze data. Group members agree to make phone calls, do library research, collect documents, and produce computer printouts. The convener and the recorder, in particular, should watch to see if group members follow through on the agreements made at team meetings. If follow through does not occur, it should be a topic of group discussion during a debriefing. Figure 7.5 illustrates how a nine-member site council sought to become an effective group.

Even though effective group dynamics are essential for cooperative action research, no text on action research has addressed their importance. Read *Learning to Work in Groups* (Miles 1981), *The Handbook of Organization Development in Schools and Colleges* (Schmuck and Runkel 1994), and *Group Processes in the Classroom* (Schmuck and Schmuck 1997) for additional tips on how to achieve effective group dynamics in schools.

A Site Council's Effective Group Dynamics

A nine-member site council of an elementary school sought to become an effective group by taking the following actions:

1. *Establish feelings of membership, inclusion, and trust.* Early in its development, the council spent a full day teambuilding with a facilitator. The teambuilding entailed get-acquainted activities, discussions about personal values and member self-concepts, simulations on group work, and the formation of group agreements about how the council will run its meetings and how it will transact business between meetings.

2. *Foster shared influence and dispersed leadership.* The council rotates roles of convener, recorder, and process observer throughout its membership from meeting to meeting. It strives to obtain agenda items from every member and to see that every member is involved continually in at least one of the council's projects.

3. *Accentuate friendliness and cohesiveness.* All meetings start with twenty minutes of check-in, during which each member shares something personal with the group. At holiday time, each member draws the name of another member out of a hat and gives that person a gift valued at less than ten dollars. Members rotate the task of bringing fruit and cookies to the meetings.

4. *Cope with social status differences.* The council agrees to monitor its participation patterns to insure that everyone gets a chance to speak and to be heard. The group agrees to use sparingly acronyms and educational jargon and to explain educational matters in plain English. Like the teachers and administrators, classified staff members and parents serve their turns as convener, recorder, and process observer.

5. *Use sound meeting skills.* In a follow up to the day of teambuilding, a facilitator trains the council in effective meeting skills.

6. *Use sound communication skills.* Also, in a follow up to the day of teambuilding, a facilitator trains the council in effective communication skills.

7. *Reach understandings about group agreements.* The council keeps a handbook in which it records its group agreements. Group agreements are made during discussions in which each member states a norm or custom that he or she would like others to practice. For example, use the STP concepts during problem solving. The council discusses each proposal until it makes the agreement.

8. *Strive to make decisions by consensus.* The council agrees that it will seek a response from every member before making a decision. If members differ, creative compromises will be brainstormed. If a minority of members cannot be completely satisfied with the decision, they are asked to go along with it for a prescribed period without sabotaging it.

9. *Take time to debrief the team's group processes.* Time is set aside at the middle of every meeting to debrief the group processes. This discussion is convened by the process observer for that session.

10. *Look to see if there is group follow through.* After check-in, the agenda for every meeting calls for a review of where the council is on each of its projects.

Figure 7.5

Seven Probing Questions to Initiate Action Research

At your next group meeting, try to follow these probing questions to initiate action research:

1. Let us start with you brainstorming issues in the school—particularly problems in teaching and learning—that you have been reflecting on lately. Tell me a little more about those problems.

2. OK, good. I heard you refer to (x) different problems. Let me try to paraphrase each one. Am I accurate?

3. Now, talk about ways in which you think these problems might be interrelated. Please tell me more about that. What would be an example? Please clarify . . .

4. Let me try to summarize what I think the problems are in teaching and learning that concern you the most. Am I accurate? Please tell me more about . . .

5. Now, let me see if I understand how you see the current situation. Let me see if I understand how you see the ideal targets you wish to strive toward. Am I accurate?

6. OK, good. Let's brainstorm the helping and hindering forces you see in the situation. What is helping you move toward your target? What is keeping you from moving toward your target? I would summarize the key forces as . . . Am I accurate?

7. Now, let us brainstorm together about the actions you might take (proactive action research) and about the data you should collect to clarify the problem (responsive action research). I hope I have helped you get a running start on your action-research project.

Ten Tips for Effective Group Dynamics

Jot down ways you can carry out each of the ten tips for effective group dynamics.

1. Establish feelings of membership, inclusion, and trust.

2. Foster shared influence and dispersed leadership.

3. Accentuate friendliness and cohesiveness.

4. Cope with social status differences.

5. Use sound meeting skills.

6. Use sound communication skills.

7. Reach understandings about group agreements.

8. Strive to make decisions by consensus.

9. Take time to debrief the team's group processes.

10. Look to see if there is group follow through.

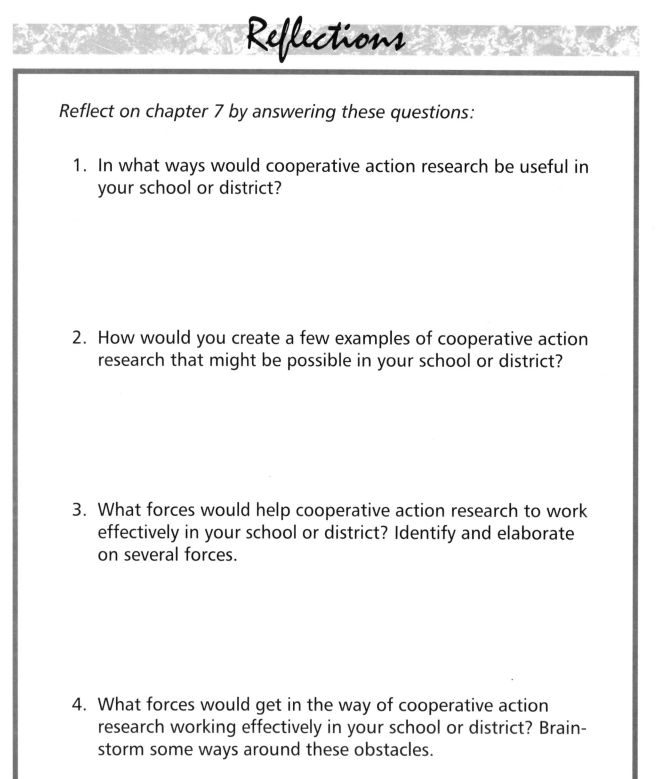

Reflections

Reflect on chapter 7 by answering these questions:

1. In what ways would cooperative action research be useful in your school or district?

2. How would you create a few examples of cooperative action research that might be possible in your school or district?

3. What forces would help cooperative action research to work effectively in your school or district? Identify and elaborate on several forces.

4. What forces would get in the way of cooperative action research working effectively in your school or district? Brainstorm some ways around these obstacles.

Chapter 8

Types of Cooperative Action Research

A promising technique for ensuring that data are converted into action is to organize the research operations so that the group to be served, the consumers of the data, are collaborators in the planning, measurement, analysis, and interpretation of the data. —Ronald Lippitt

The exercise of reinventing the wheel can provide an important opportunity for staff to work through and understand project precepts . . . without this learning by doing it is doubtful that projects attempting to achieve teacher change would be effectively implemented.
—Paul Berman and Milbrey McLaughlin

Fifty years ago, Ron Lippitt described the power of cooperative action research by summing up how to improve community relations. Later, Paul Berman and Milbrey McLaughlin (1975), coauthoring *Federal Programs Supporting Educational Change,* showed how effective innovation in classrooms depended on active cooperation of local teachers and administrators in designing, implementing, and evaluating a tailored change for their own school.

Cooperative action research can be carried out at different system levels of the school district, from one-on-one partnerships to districtwide networks of educators and their community stakeholders. Following are different ways action research can be conducted under different circumstances and detailed examples of educators conducting cooperative action research.

One-on-One Partnerships

One-on-one partnerships occur frequently in individual action-research projects when one person advises or mentors another. Examples of such collaboration were presented in chapters 5 and 6. One-on-one partnerships also occur when two people work together on a single cooperative action research effort. Figure 8.1 lists Typical One-on-One Partnerships.

Small Face-to-Face Groups

Most cooperative action research takes place in small work groups with three to ten members. These groups are characterized by task interdependence and regular face-to-face meetings. To be effective in implementing all steps of cooperative

Typical One-on-One Partnerships

1. A teacher and a teacher

   - A kindergarten teacher and a first grade teacher perform action research to help students move from preschool to first grade

   - A fifth grade teacher and a second grade teacher do action research in a cross-age tutoring program

   - Two senior high math teachers focus on making algebra and trigonometry interesting to their students

   - An English teacher pairs with a social studies teacher to do research on an effective division of labor to teach students to write well

2. A teacher and a student

   - A fourth grade teacher and a special-needs student use action research to help improve the student's reading skills

   - A sixth grade teacher and a student with an attention deficit explore classroom activities that help the student stay on task

   - A middle school teacher and a student find alternative settings for doing homework

   - A high school coach and an athlete find a balance between athletics and academics

3. A counselor and a student

   - A counselor and a foreign-born third grader use action research to help the student understand the elementary school's culture

   - A counselor and an aggressive fourth grader learn how to curb the student's tendency to start fights

   - A counselor pairs with a middle school student to find ways to deal with the student's feelings of isolation

   - A counselor and a twelfth grader determine signs of sexism and racism in the school

4. An administrator and a teacher

   - An administrator and a second grade teacher study alternative ways to engage senior citizens as classroom assistants

   - An administrator and a fifth grade teacher find alternative ways to increase students' time on task

   - An administrator and a teacher responsible for the student council convince students to take constructive action for school improvement

   - An administrator and a high school counselor study how to help students determine what they will do after graduation

Figure 8.1

action research, the members must communicate clearly with one another, understand the primary purposes of the research, run efficient meetings, solve problems together, make decisions about steps of the project that are acceptable to everyone, work constructively and creatively with conflicts, and value differences within the group. Figure 8.2 lists Typical Small Face-to-Face Groups.

Whole School Staffs

Compared to small face-to-face groups with no more than two levels of authority, whole school staffs have three or more levels of authority and are more complex. Often, because of the size of a whole staff, a school's site council serves as a surrogate of the whole and becomes the locus of schoolwide action research. Other times, as illustrated below, the whole staff cooperates in action research. When that happens, the whole staff is engaged simultaneously in cooperative action research, organization development, and school improvement.

Proactive Projects

Whole staffs engage in cooperative, proactive action research when they participate in

Typical Small Face-to-Face Groups

1. One educator (a teacher, a counselor, or an administrator) with a few students drawn from different classrooms and grade levels

   - An upper-elementary teacher cooperates with a small group of fourth, fifth, and sixth graders to study how students of that school can effectively serve a nearby senior citizens' center

   - An elementary counselor and a small group of student representatives learn how to reduce, mediate, and manage student conflicts on the playground, in the halls, in the lunchroom, and on the way to and from school

   - A middle school counselor and a small group of eighth and ninth graders help seventh graders feel comfortable, included, and secure in the school

   - A high school principal and student leaders learn about managing unsportsmanlike behaviors of students and parents at competitive sports events

2. Collegial teams of teachers from different grade levels or diverse disciplines

   - A fourth, a fifth, and a sixth grade teacher do action research on establishing, training, and managing student steering committees in their classrooms

   - Four middle school teachers with expertise in English, social studies, science, and math develop interdisciplinary learning projects for eighth graders

   - Five high school teachers with primary responsibility for tenth graders implement writing across the curriculum

   - Six elementary teachers from each grade level find new ways to report students' academic performance to parents

3. Mixed intraschool teams of teachers, counselors, specialists, and administrators with responsibility to represent their colleagues

   - Two special educators and two regular fourth grade teachers research ways to include special-needs students in classroom activities

   - An administrator, two special educators, a counselor, and two teachers find alternative methods for profiling student achievement in several curriculum areas

   - Seven teachers, each from a different elementary school, explore ways to prepare sixth graders for middle school

   - Eight administrators, each from a different secondary school, discover ways to improve the quality of large faculty meetings

4. Site councils or intraschool governing teams with educators, classified staff members, and parents

   - The site council of an elementary school does cooperative action research to establish and maintain clear and open channels of communication between itself and the school's stakeholders

   - A middle school site council researches alternative methods of classroom management

   - A high school site council finds ways to reduce racism and prejudice within the student body

   - A middle school site council studies a course in communication skills for seventh graders

5. School boards from districts with diverse ethnic groups and people from all walks of life

   - The school board of a small rural district does research to write a policy on homework

   - A suburban school board, with a rapidly declining budget, studies how to fund extracurricular activities

   - An urban school board studies how to improve teachers' morale

Figure 8.2

IRI/SkyLight Training and Publishing, Inc.

schoolwide inservice workshops, school-based staff development, and organization-development training. Such events aim to bring about school improvements in teamwork, student learning, staff morale, and school climate. After the events, data are collected to help plan the future, and the cycle of steps in proactive action research unfold. See Figure 8.3 for different ways a school staff might engage in proactive action research.

Responsive Projects

Whole school staffs engage in cooperative, responsive action research when they complete needs assessments, fill out school-climate questionnaires, hold probing conversations about the strengths and shortcomings of the school's program, or formally observe interactions at staff meetings, in one another's classes, and at extra-

curricular events. Once collected and analyzed, the data give impetus to new practices, and the cycle of steps in responsive action research unfold. See Figure 8.3 for ways a staff might launch responsive action research.

Districtwide Educator Networks and Stakeholders

Although school boards usually link educators with stakeholders in the community, the superintendent and board members sometimes put together an educator-stakeholder task force to tackle a specific problem. Such a task force can make good use of cooperative action research. See Figure 8.4 for reasons districts might establish

Whole School Staff Action Research

Proactive Action Research

Whole school staffs might engage in proactive action research to do the following:

- Assess student learning in a curriculum domain
- Improve the social-emotional climate of the staff
- Increase clear communication with parents
- Enhance inclusion of special-needs students in regular classrooms
- Improve the quality of staff meetings and staff development
- Increase cooperation and social support between staff and students
- Enhance students' willingness and skill in facilitating their peers' academic performance
- Improve communication channels between the whole staff and the site council
- Increase abilities of teachers and students to participate effectively in cooperative learning

Responsive Action Research

Whole school staffs might launch responsive action research to do the following:

- Assess staff members' thoughts and feelings about their own learning needs
- Check on the feelings of inclusion or alienation among staff members, students, and parents
- Diagnose teachers' perceptions and feelings about the school's administrative leadership
- Assess students' understanding and performance of academic tasks
- Check staff members' reactions to group problem solving at faculty meetings
- Diagnose students' attitudes toward different teaching methods
- Assess parents' attitudes toward the school's performing arts program
- Check teachers' reactions to how administrators are implementing district policy on teacher supervision and evaluation
- Diagnose students' views about sexism and racism in the school

Figure 8.3

educator-stakeholder task forces to carry out action research.

Case Studies

Cooperative action research can be carried out in various ways. The cases below illustrate eight alternatives—four are proactive action research and four are responsive action research. They do not constitute an exhaustive list of possibilities.

*One-on-One Partnership**

Robyn Mills and Irene Oswald decide to implement a cross-age tutoring program at Franklin Elementary. Robyn and Irene learn about cross-age tutoring in a university course and conversations with teachers using it. Robyn's fifth graders will be trained to tutor Irene's second graders in math for twenty minutes three times a week. Robyn and Irene cooperate in proactive action research to prepare training programs for the fifth and second graders.

Step 1: Try a New Practice

Robyn and Irene take five days to prepare their respective students for cross-age tutoring. They pair the fifth and second graders according to their interpersonal compatibility and implement initial tutoring sessions three days a week for twenty minutes a day. Robin and Irene spend twenty minutes with their own students on Fridays and Mondays to debrief them on the progress of the tutoring and ways to improve it.

Step 2: Incorporate Hopes and Concerns

Robyn and Irene agree on the following hopes for cross-age tutoring:

- Increase second graders' knowledge and skill in math
- Enhance fifth graders' motivation and interest in math
- Foster cross-age empathy and friendship in the school
- Encourage fifth graders to take responsibility for second graders' behavior to enhance the social behavior of fifth graders

Robyn and Irene also brainstorm their concerns for what could go wrong:

- A few second graders will be unresponsive tutees
- A few fifth graders will not consider tutoring to be fun or worthwhile

---

Educator-Stakeholder Task Forces

During the past decade, many districts have been compelled to reduce their budgets and eliminate parts of programs. Some districts have formed special educator-stakeholder committees to advise the board on how to make the cuts. Other districts might establish educator-stakeholder task forces to carry out action research to do the following:

- Enhance the district's capacity to use computers effectively
- Improve the district's standing in its community
- Increase senior citizens' participation in school programs

- Assess citizens' perceptions of the district's strengths and shortcomings
- Check local business people's perceptions of the employability of high school graduates
- Diagnose why a majority of citizens voted against constructing a new high school

Figure 8.4

---

*All names of educators, schools, and communities have been changed.

- Some fifth graders will not give accurate math information to their tutees

- A few parents of fifth graders will complain that cross-age tutoring keeps their youngsters from learning their own fifth grade math

Step 3: Collect Data

After the tutoring takes place for two weeks, Robyn and Irene separately collect data from one another's students. Robyn interviews second graders as an entire class. Irene conducts whole-group interviews with fifth graders. Robyn and Irene tell students they want to determine what is going well and what needs improvement in the tutoring. They ask students to sit in a large circle and speak one after the other around the circle. The students explain one good thing about the tutoring and one thing that could be improved. At the end of each group interview, Robyn and Irene ask students to complete individually the following sentences:

1. My tutoring partner's name is . . .

2. Compared with other ways to learn math, working with a partner is . . .

3. For me, math is . . .

4. About math, my tutoring partner feels . . .

On the following Monday, Robyn and Irene give their own students a math test.

Step 4: Check What the Data Mean

Robyn and Irene analyze the group interviews and sentence-completion items. On Monday, they discuss their data analyses and the math test scores. From the interviews, Robyn and Irene compose a list of what is going well and what needs improvement in the tutoring. For the sentence completions, Robyn and Irene keep a five-point evaluation scale in mind to judge how many responses are highly positive, positive, neutral, negative, and highly negative. They also score the math tests for accuracy. Then, they brainstorm ideas about what the various data mean. They decide to bring the two classes together to discuss how to improve the tutoring.

Step 5: Reflect on Alternative Ways to Behave

Robyn and Irene bring their classes to the media-resource center. They explain that the data show most students feel positively toward tutoring; although, a few wish for change. Robyn and Irene take turns stating what is going well in tutoring and what needs improvement. As they go through the two lists, they stop several times to ask student pairs to generate additional ideas.

A few days later, Robyn and Irene bring their classes together again. This time they discuss four problems that need to be solved to improve the tutoring:

- Twenty minutes is often not enough time for effective math tutoring

- Some second graders do not do the homework assigned by their tutors

- Some fifth graders act too tough and are not patient

- Some tutoring pairs do not stay on task

Robyn and Irene ask the pairs to brainstorm ways to solve these four problems. They print lists of the students' ideas on poster paper.

Step 6: Try Another New Practice

Robyn and Irene tell their students the tutoring will be postponed for a week so that improvements can be made. They explain that while the tutoring has been successful, there are still a few important ways that it can be improved. They each work separately with their own classes.

Robyn has fifth graders role-play the tutoring relationship in pairs. She teaches the students to use different forms of positive reinforcement and social support. She alternates her direct instruction with role-playing and coaches the fifth graders on realistic homework assignments for second graders.

Irene uses pairs of second graders as part of her instruction. She asks pairs to practice math problems together, both in class and after school, to emphasize the importance of practicing math skills over and over. She has pairs discuss how they will meet to do math homework and urges them to spend fifteen minutes a day doing math problems together outside class. Irene also coaches second graders on ways to speak up to fifth graders when they feel insecure.

Robyn and Irene combine their classes again for a meeting. They ask students to sit together in tutoring pairs. Robyn summarizes what she did with fifth graders, and Irene summarizes what she did with second graders. Then, they ask tutoring pairs to brainstorm ways to stay on the task of learning math. On the following day, cross-age tutoring resumes. Robyn and Irene continue the cross-age tutoring for the rest of the school year; subsequent data show that the results are positive. (Read "Cross-Age Relationships: An Educational Resource," Lippitt and Lohman [1965], for ideas on how to use cross-age relationships to increase student learning.)

Small Face-to-Face Groups (One Educator with Students)*

During the four years he has been a counselor at McKinley Middle School (grades 7–9), John Mack has been impressed with the number of seventh graders who come to him for help with social-emotional problems. He decides to ask eight student leaders (two eighth grade girls, two eighth grade boys, two ninth grade girls, and two ninth grade boys) to cooperate with him on action research to find ways to help McKinley's seventh graders feel included and secure.

John invites the eight students to eat lunch with him in the cafeteria. He tells them about his experiences with seventh graders and his desire to do action research on the problem. Then, John leads the students through a series of team-building activities to help them become better acquainted before launching the action research together. John tells the students about how responsive action research works.

Step 1: Collect Data

John and the eight students conduct one-on-one interviews with 72 of the 144 seventh graders at

McKinley. Each member of the action-research team, including John, agrees to interview eight seventh graders randomly selected from a class list. Each interview is scheduled for thirty minutes during a school day. The interviews take place over two and one-half weeks.

Prior to the interviews, John, the principal, and the eight student action researchers meet with all of the seventh graders in the gym. The principal talks briefly about the value of a positive school climate. John introduces the idea of a cooperative action-research project and the team of eight students who will work with him. John explains the first step—the one-on-one interviews—and the importance of every seventh grader participating. He explains that participation in the interviews is voluntary.

Step 2: Analyze the Data

After the interviews, John and the student team agree on a strategy to analyze the data. They decide to construct lists of concrete examples from answers to questions 1, 2, and 6. (See Figure 8.5 for the Questions for One-on-One Interviews.) For question 3, they tally the number of times that better, about the same, and less occur for each elementary "feeder" school (McKinley receives students from three elementary schools). For question 4, they give each interviewee a number and construct lists of all interviewees' extracurricular activities. For question 5, they give each interviewee a simple yes or no and try to discern reasons for no responses. Figure 8.6 lists the Themes in the Data that the action-research team found.

Step 3: Distribute the Data and Announce Changes

John asks seventh grade social studies teachers if his research team can use forty minutes of social studies time to feed data back to students. John gets approval to visit five social studies classes on one day, giving the researchers an opportunity to speak to all 144 seventh graders. The eight students on John's team form into pairs, each pair

---

*All names of educators, schools, and communities have been changed.

Questions for One-on-One Interviews

1. Tell me what you like most about McKinley Middle School. (Probe for concrete examples.)

2. Tell me what you do not like about McKinley Middle School. (Probe for concrete examples.)

3. Which elementary school did you attend before coming to McKinley? Do you like McKinley better, about the same, or less? Please explain your answer.

4. Outside of your regular classes, are you participating in any extracurricular activities at McKinley? If yes, which ones?

5. Do your best friends attend McKinley or another school?

6. What sorts of changes at McKinley would help you feel better about going to school here? (Probe for concrete examples.)

Figure 8.5

Themes in the Data

High points of the data reveal the following themes:

- Things liked most about McKinley are the competitive after-school sports (as spectators), the teachers, school spirit at pep rallies, and the food choices

- Things liked least about McKinley are the big and impersonal school, the homework, eighth and ninth graders sticking among themselves, and how hard it is to get on school athletic teams

- Students from the smallest and most rural elementary school—much more than students from the other two elementary schools—like McKinley less than their elementary school

- Only 10 percent of seventh graders interviewed participate in extracurricular activities at McKinley—most are boys

- About 80 percent of interviewees have best friends at McKinley; many of the 20 percent who do not come from the smallest, most rural elementary school

- The changes that would make seventh graders feel better about McKinley are more opportunities to get to know other students, more common activities with eighth and ninth graders, seventh grade competitive after-school sports, and teachers giving more reasonable amounts of homework

Figure 8.6

gives data feedback to one of four social studies classes. John gives feedback to the fifth class.

At the feedback sessions, the researchers summarize data from step 2 and describe some changes that will probably be tried (see Figure 8.7 for the list of changes).

During the last ten minutes of each feedback session, the researchers divide the seventh graders into trios. They ask these trios to give their reactions to the ideas for change and to brainstorm additional ideas for improving student life at McKinley.

Step 4: Try a New Practice

The principal launches cross-grade-level miniassemblies immediately. He holds one a week

for seven weeks to address all of McKinley's students. On the eighth week, the principal leads an all-student-body assembly, during which he announces various ways cohesiveness is being increased among the seventh, eighth, and ninth graders.

John works with the PE department to run indoor intramural soccer games. Each soccer team comprises three seventh graders, three eighth graders, and three ninth graders. The eight student leaders on the research team volunteer to referee games in pairs.

The soccer, basketball, and track coaches initiate meetings with their counterparts in five nearby schools to discuss the feasibility of seventh grade competitive after-school sports.

Changes for McKinley

- The principal leads a series of cross-grade-level miniassemblies in the library. Twenty seventh graders, twenty eighth graders, and twenty ninth graders attend each miniassembly. The topic is how to increase cohesiveness of the McKinley student body.

- The PE department launches a program of intramural sports at McKinley. Each team comprise equal numbers of seventh, eighth, and ninth graders.

- McKinley's coaches discuss the possibility of seventh grade competitive after-school sports.

- John leads teachers in a problem-solving discussion about McKinley's homework policy, its current implementation, and ways to improve both.

Figure 8.7

John convenes teachers at several faculty meetings to discuss homework. The discussions reveal that the amount of homework differs greatly from one teacher to another. The teachers decide to try to keep each of their homework assignments to about twenty minutes per day for the seventh graders.

Step 5: Check Others' Reactions

John and the student leaders continue to meet as an action-research team for fifty minutes once a week. Between these meetings, they collect data as follows: After dividing the 144 seventh graders by nine, each member of the research team, including John, informally observes and interviews his or her cluster of sixteen seventh graders. The observations focus on participation in miniassemblies, intramural soccer, and mingling in the hallways before, during, and after school. They look for indications that the seventh graders are interacting with eighth and ninth graders more, the same, or less than they were before the new actions. The informal interviews focus on seventh graders' perceptions and feelings about the new actions. When the researchers discuss their observations and interviews at their meetings, they seek ways to fine-tune the new actions.

Step 6: Collect Data

After the new actions have been carried out for fifteen weeks, John and the student team construct a questionnaire to administer to all seventh graders. The questionnaire has six items to be

answered with a five-point Likert scale. See Figure 8.8 for the Special Survey of McKinley's Seventh Graders questionnaire.

Small Face-to-Face Groups* (Collegial Teacher Teams)

Brentwood High School's principal joins five of her teachers at a statewide conference on writing across the curriculum. Since Mary Dunlap (English) and Bruce Monson (world history) were already cooperating on their writing assignments for tenth graders, the two of them asked Terri Gates (biology), Frank Leeber (geometry), and Francoise Garcia (French and Spanish) to go to the conference with them and the principal. At the conference, the new team decides to try proactive action research with writing across the curriculum for the tenth graders.

Step 1: Try a New Practice

The team decides that each member will assign writing to his or her tenth graders one day a week. Francoise chooses Monday, Frank chooses Tuesday, Terri chooses Wednesday, and Bruce and Mary choose Thursday and Friday, respectively. The team of five meets once a week to discuss its new practice.

Step 2: Incorporate Hopes and Concerns

The team agrees on the following hopes for writing across the curriculum:

All names of educators, schools, and communities have been changed.

Special Survey of McKinley's Seventh Graders

Please circle one answer next to each item to show whether you strongly agree, agree, feel neutral, disagree, or strongly disagree (SA, A, N, D, SD).

1. The principal's miniassemblies with seventh, eighth, and ninth graders have helped me meet upper-grade students.
   SA   A   N   D   SD

2. The indoor intramural soccer program helps seventh, eighth, and ninth graders get to know one another better.
   SA   A   N   D   SD

3. The amount of homework I must do is more reasonable now than it was earlier in the year.
   SA   A   N   D   SD

4. I would like to see McKinley's seventh graders compete against seventh graders from other schools in track and field this coming spring.
   SA   A   N   D   SD

5. I think McKinley's seventh graders should compete against seventh graders from other schools in soccer next fall.
   SA   A   N   D   SD

6. I think McKinley's seventh graders should compete against seventh graders from other schools in basketball next fall.
   SA   A   N   D   SD

7. Other changes I would like to see at McKinley are _____

   _____

   _____

   _____

Figure 8.8

- Help students see that good writing is important in all subjects

- Impress young tenth graders about the importance of writing well

- Upgrade students' writing skills through multiple feedback channels

The team also discusses its concerns for what might go wrong:

- Some students might complain about too much writing

- Teachers might assign writing as homework too much and not have students write in class enough

- Teachers might shortchange other skills because so much attention is given to writing well

To cope with the possibility that these concerns might come true, the team decides the following:

- Each teacher tells his or her students at least once a week about the importance of learning to write well

- Only Mary and Bruce assign writing for homework, and they will alternate that from week to week

- Once every three weeks, the team discusses how well students seem to be learning the curriculum each teacher offers

Step 3: Collect Data

After six weeks, the team collects data on the effects of its cooperative effort. Francoise and Terri prepare a questionnaire to assess the tenth graders' attitudes toward writing. Frank gives a test in geometry in which students must write answers in sentences and paragraphs. Mary and Bruce score a sample of students' written work for its grammatical quality. All five ask tenth graders to write a paragraph on their feelings about each class.

Step 4: Check What the Data Mean

Each teacher analyzes the data he or she has collected. Frank creates a spreadsheet with student names and scores on attitudes and tests.

Mary and Bruce do a content analysis of the most common weaknesses in students' writing. Terri and Francoise do a content analysis of the students' feelings toward the five classes. The team meets twice during the eighth week to discuss what the data mean.

Step 5: Reflect on Alternative Ways to Behave

Frank's spreadsheet shows that girls have more positive attitudes toward writing than boys. In geometry, girls' test scores (when writing answers in prose) are higher than those of boys. The team urges Frank to have boys in his class work in critical-friendship pairs or in helping trios to get them more involved in writing. Mary and Bruce find that quite a few students write better in English class than they do in world history and biology.

Mary, Bruce, and Terri decide to trade writing samples from their classes with one another during the next three weeks. Francoise and Terri find that students feel most negative about writing in French and Spanish. The team decides to focus writing assignments for the next six weeks on English, world history, biology, and geometry. Francoise primarily emphasizes oral skills in French and Spanish.

Step 6: Try Another New Practice

The team presents a panel on the program to students and their parents. The principal convenes it, emphasizing the centrality of good writing for student success in school and in life. Each of the five teachers presents part of the information from steps 4 and 5 of the action research. They end by describing changes they will make to improve the program and by reaffirming their common commitment to good writing. The principal leads the parents and students in a question-and-answer session about the tenth grade curriculum at Brentwood. All participants are pleased with the effectiveness of the new writing program.

Small Face-to-Face Groups* (Mixed Educator Team)

Richard Byers (counselor) and Rebecca Stein (English) chat one day about their mutual concern for negative interpersonal events among Firgrove High School students. They have both heard students complain about one another, their teachers, and a couple of administrators. Nancy Wong (social studies) joins Richard and Rebecca to say that she has heard quite a few anti-Asian statements from the students lately. Richard tells Rebecca and Nancy about a few fistfights between Caucasian and Asian boys. Rebecca adds that Bob Leaburg (coach and physical education) told her about anti-Asian sentiments he overheard among the football players. Bob Leaburg sees the other three in conversation. He confirms what Rebecca said. The four decide to talk about their shared concerns with Joann Robinson (principal).

When Joann hears the concerns of the four teachers, she tells them she shares their worries. She invites them to join her in an effort to reduce anti-Asian prejudice at Firgrove and to improve school climate. Nancy tells the group about responsive action research. All agree to cooperate for the rest of the academic year in research to improve the social climate for everyone in the school and, in particular, to try to reduce anti-Asian prejudice. Joann announces the project to the whole staff, inviting others to communicate their perceptions to Richard Byers, who will serve as chair of the responsive action-research team.

Step 1: Collect Data

The research team agrees with Nancy's idea to collect data via questionnaires, interviews, and observations. Drawing information from a college course, Richard introduces a questionnaire titled Student Questionnaire on Organizational Functioning, which assesses student perceptions of conflict, communication, decision making, and responsiveness between teachers and students, among the students, and among the teachers (see Schmuck and Schmuck 1997, pp. 249–251). The

All names of educators, schools, and communities have been changed.

team tailors the questionnaire to Firgrove by modifying its language and by adding a few questions about prejudices and discrimination. Joann suggests that data be collected in English classes, since all Firgrove students are required to take English every semester.

Nancy and Rebecca agree to work together in Rebecca's journalism class to train students to interview samples of students and staff about instances of racism and prejudice at Firgrove.

Joann, Richard, and Bob agree to create a form for structured observations in the hallways, at lunch, and at assemblies and sports events. All five team members volunteer to act as participant observers in those different behavior settings during the next few weeks.

Step 2: Analyze the Data

Data from questionnaires, summarized by Richard on spreadsheets, clearly show that students perceive high conflict within the student body. What surprises the team is the high number of students who do not think the principal or the teachers care about student conflicts. In fact, almost half of the students do not believe that the principal will listen to them or that teachers really want to help students with their problems.

Results from the journalism students' interviews highlight several intergroup tensions. One concerns open conflict between male athletes and male Asian Americans. The interviewers point out, mainly from their observations during interviews, that few male Asian Americans are on the sports teams and that the male Asian Americans typically are better academic students than the male athletes. A second tension shows up between socially oriented females, who hang around the male athletes, and academically oriented females, who tend to run the school's music and theater projects. Teacher observations adhere to the findings of the journalism students.

Step 3: Distribute the Data and Announce Changes

The research team believes that the first and most important target for data feedback and change is

the Firgrove faculty. Team members think that the faculty has to change its relationships with students, if students are to change their relationships with one another. The team forms into a panel to feed back data at a faculty meeting. Faculty members agree that they are part of the problem and would like that to change.

Joann tells the faculty that she has the superintendent's permission and the school board's approval to cancel school on the Wednesday before Thanksgiving so the faculty can retreat together. She describes a facility in the countryside near Firgrove where the faculty will go on Tuesday after school and have time to work together until Wednesday afternoon. The main issue for the retreat is how to turn around negative energy at Firgrove and how to show students that the faculty is concerned about students as human beings. Joann ends the session by telling the faculty that the action-research team will hire a neutral facilitator to run the retreat.

Step 4: Try a New Practice

Joann, Richard, and Nancy summarize the team's data for the facilitator. The facilitator uses the STP paradigm for problem solving (Schmuck and Runkel 1994, pp. 229–65). The basic idea is that a problem is a gap between an unsatisfactory current situation (S) and a more desirable goal or target (T). The problem is solved, or reduced, when a path or plan (P) is found from S to T. See Figure 8.9 for the facilitator's assessment of Firgrove's Problems.

The facilitator commences the retreat with a few warm-up activities and a group exercise to demonstrate how to cooperate in problem-solving groups. Next, she leads the five problem-solving groups (each with nine faculty members and a facilitator from the action-research team) through the first five steps of the STP paradigm:

1. Specify the problem
2. List helping and hindering forces
3. Specify multiple solutions
4. Plan for action
5. Anticipate obstacles

Firgrove's Problems

The facilitator defines Firgrove's problems as the following:

- The situation (S) is that male athletes and male Asian Americans are engaged in unproductive conflict; the target (T) is for male athletes and male Asian Americans to feel friendly toward one another.

- The situation (S) is that some socially oriented females and some academically oriented females are engaged in unproductive conflict. The target (T) is for both groups to feel friendly toward one another.

- The situation (S) is that many students think the administration does not care about student conflicts at Firgrove. The target (T) is for students to believe the administrators are sensitive to their concerns and are trying to reduce student conflict at Firgrove.

- The situation (S) is that many students think most teachers do not care about reducing student conflicts at Firgrove. The target (T) is for students to believe that most teachers do care about their concerns and are trying to reduce student conflicts at Firgrove.

- The situation (S) is that the Firgrove faculty has no procedure for assessing students' concerns. The target (T) is for the Firgrove faculty to institutionalize procedures for both assessing and acting on student concerns.

Figure 8.9

By Wednesday afternoon, each small group is ready to present its action plan to the whole faculty. After the action plans are presented, the facilitator asks each group to nominate one person to work with the action-research team member to coordinate the follow through of its action plan. The new group of coordinators meets with the facilitator to discuss the next steps. Figure 8.10 outlines some of these Action Ideas.

Action Ideas

A few action ideas from each problem-solving group are as follows:

Group 1: Get key leaders of the male athletes and the male Asian Americans to run a school carnival together to raise funds for the school's media center. Have Richard and Nancy run a constructive confrontation with a sample of male athletes and a sample of male Asian Americans.

Group 2: Get key leaders of the socially oriented females and the academically oriented females to do STP problem solving together on the target of a supportive social-emotional climate for everyone. Have Bob and Rebecca run a series of brief get-better-acquainted activities with female students who are members of different informal subgroups.

Group 3: Have Joann visit every team, club, or other extracurricular group during the next month to listen to student concerns. The administrative team runs an annual questionnaire survey of students on some aspect of school climate.

Group 4: Assign every teacher an "advisee group" of students to counsel and mentor for thirty minutes twice a week. All English and social studies teachers present units on racism and prejudice during the next two months.

Group 5: This group also came up with the ideas of an annual survey of students and of advisee groups for every teacher. It suggests, too, that the outside facilitator, who led the Firgrove faculty at the retreat, should carry out STP problem solving with heterogeneous groups of male and female students on reducing racism and prejudice among the students.

Figure 8.10

Step 5: Check Others' Reactions

The newly formed team of ten coordinators (two from each problem-solving group) decides to track faculty reactions to the retreat. Each coordinator interviews three or four colleagues about their attitudes toward the retreat and what, if anything, they are doing differently. Rebecca and Nancy ask the journalism students to do a story about the retreat and its aftermath for the school newspaper. Bob includes character and social responsibility in his meetings with male athletes. Richard and Joann make a special effort to interview a sample of Asian-American students.

Step 6: Collect Data

Toward the end of April, that same academic year, the team of ten coordinators replicates the data collection of the preceding fall. Results show an improved school climate at Firgrove.

Small Face-to-Face Groups* (Site Council)

Burney Elementary School (K–7), a large elementary school with thirty-six certified teachers, is organized into four teams: K–1, with seven regular teachers and three special educators; grades 2–3, with six regular teachers and three special educators; grades 4–5, with seven regular teachers and two special educators; grades 6–7, with seven regular teachers and one special educator.

Burney is governed by a site council with nine members—four regular teachers (one from each team), one special educator (from the K–1 team), one classified staff member (a custodian), two parents, and the principal. After a series of three training sessions in communication and meeting skills, the site council feels it's ready to communicate with Burney's stakeholders.

Step 1: Try a New Practice

Acting on advice from the superintendent, the principal asks each site-council member to serve as a communication link between the council and Burney's stakeholders. The principal links with the assistant principal, office staff members, and district-office administrators. Each regular teacher links with members of his or her teaching team. The special educator helps each teacher link with special educators on each team. The custodian links with cooks, bus drivers, and one other custodian. The two parents take on the formidable task of linking to the Burney parents. The principal pledges to help the two parents find effective ways to communicate with other parents.

The new practice at Burney is an organizational structure for communication and decision making. Burney is to be a representative democracy in which the site council—as the primary governing body—strives to maintain communication channels between itself and its stakeholders.

Step 2: Incorporate Hopes and Concerns

The site council agrees on the following hopes for itself:

- Make decisions and take actions that enhance student learning

- Solve problems cooperatively and make decisions consensually

- Maintain clear communication channels with stakeholders

- Lead in making Burney a healthy environment for students and staff

- Establish strong ties with parents and other citizens in the Burney community

Later, the site council spends an entire meeting brainstorming what the members believe could go wrong:

- Reaching consensus might be difficult

- Might lose sight of students as we become engaged with one another

- Maintaining effective two-way communication with stakeholders might be difficult

- Getting a lot of parents involved in the school might be challenging

---

All names of educators, schools, and communities have been changed.

Step 3: Collect Data

After functioning together for three months, the site council divides itself into three subgroups with three members each to collect different sorts of data. Subgroup 1 (two teachers and the special educator) collects data from students. Subgroup 2 (two teachers and the custodian) collects data from the staff. Subgroup 3 (two parents and the principal) collects data from the parents.

Subgroup 1 uses questionnaires to collect attitudinal data from the students; it also asks every teacher to rate his or her students on academic-performance dimensions. Subgroup 2 decides to interview a sample of staff members about their perceptions of and attitudes toward the site council. Each member of the subgroup interviews six Burney staff members. The entire sample of eighteen is made up of twelve teachers (three from each team), the assistant principal, and five classified staff members. Subgroup 3 mails a simple one-page questionnaire to all parents to assess the parents' awareness of, knowledge of, and attitudes toward the site council.

Step 4: Check What the Data Mean

The site council meets a month later to discuss the data. Subgroup 1 finds that Burney students are happy with school and that teachers rate 85 percent of Burney students as doing "well enough" in their academic learning and social development. Two issues emerge from the data that impress the three members of the subgroup:

- As students move through fifth, sixth, and seventh grades, they tend to become increasingly more negative toward school

- Most of the bottom 15 percent of students, who the teachers rate low in learning and social development, are boys in the fifth and sixth grades

Subgroup 2 finds that fourteen of eighteen interviewees perceive the site council as being too separated and set off from the rest of the staff. Seven of fourteen use the term "elitist" to describe the site council. Ten of fourteen refer

directly to lack of communication between their representative and themselves. The lack of communication is pronounced between the site council and both the 6–7 team and classified personnel. Interviewees happiest with the site council are the K–1 and 2–3 teams.

Subgroup 3 receives only 20 percent of parent questionnaires. The data indicate that most of that 20 percent are aware of the site council and their attitudes toward it vary from neutral to positive. Members of subgroup 3 decide that a 20 percent return rate is much too low and that probably most parents know very little about the site council.

Step 5: Reflect on Alternative Ways to Behave

The Burney site council invites an expert on site councils from the state department to help it find alternative ways to build communication channels to its stakeholders. The consultant leads the nine-member council through problem solving, brainstorming, and action planning. See Figure 8.11 for the Results of the Site Council Working with the Expert.

Step 6: Try Another New Practice

Over the rest of the school year, the site council puts ideas from step 5 into action. By year's end, the site council has opened communication channels between itself and its stakeholders, and many more parents are taking part in Burney activities and programs.

Small Face-to-Face Groups (School Board)*

In the rural district of Pearton, the school board's seven members discuss their concerns about the lack of homework teachers assign students. In this district of 3,200 students, the homework issue goes back to the former superintendent who moved Pearton to a policy of no homework. Now that a new superintendent has been hired, the Pearton board decides to bring up the homework

---

All names of educators, schools, and communities have been changed.

Results of the Site Council Working with the Expert

The following ideas emerged from the site council working with the site-council expert:

- The seven site-council members who are Burney staff members will divide up each of their stakeholder groups in a new way. Instead of using formal criteria of membership to teams or to official roles in the school, the seven members will each choose five or six colleagues with whom they have frequent contact. For example, some Burney staff members drive to and from school together, see one another on weekends, attend university extension classes together, attend the same church, or have lunch together.

- The two parents and the principal will invite the parents who returned the questionnaire to a special problem-solving meeting. The goal of the meeting will be to establish parent-to-parent communication channels, such as neighborhood get-togethers, a telephone or e-mail network, and parent interest groups.

- The nine-member site council will talk about itself within a fishbowl seating arrangement at an all-staff meeting at Burney. Empty chairs will be placed within the fishbowl so that members of the audience can enter the discussion to ask questions or to contribute ideas. The agenda will be to review key issues that the Burney site council is working on.

- The Burney site council will recommend that the staff considers reorganizing itself into a "matrix structure." At present, the organizational structure works vertically. The teams and classified staff are separated from one another in the current structure. The challenge will be to develop cross-team and cross-classified personnel committees that will increase horizontal communication. Such cross-staff horizontal committees might focus on problems such as older students are more negative toward school than the younger students and boys have more learning problems than girls.

Figure 8.11

policy again. The new superintendent tells the board that a homework policy could be an appropriate topic for responsive action research.

Step 1: Collect Data

Board members and the superintendent arrange to collect three sets of data about homework: questionnaire data from parents, interview data from superintendents of rural districts, and document data on what research says about homework and student learning.

The questionnaire, one mailed to each Pearton family with children in school, is titled Parent Attitudes toward Student Homework from School. After a brief introductory paragraph about homework, the questionnaire starts with the following question:

> About our child's (children's) homework from school, we would like the teachers to assign (please answer one):

a. much more than now

b. more than now

c. the same

d. less than now

e. much less than now

The respondents are asked to elaborate on their answer to the question in order to help board members and the superintendent understand the respondents' reasoning.

Each board member talks by telephone with superintendents of five rural districts about their homework policies. Each interview lasts about fifteen minutes. After the interviewer introduces herself or himself as a Pearton board member and comments on the board's interest in homework policies, he or she asks, "Do you have a homework policy in your school district?" If yes: "Please describe your policy" and "Will you please send me a copy?" If no: "Please tell me whether teachers give homework." And finally, the interviewer uses a few probes, such as, "Can you give me an example?" or "Please tell me more about that."

A Pearton principal volunteers to do library research on homework and student learning.

Step 2: Analyze the Data

The school board gets an 80 percent return on the questionnaires. The rate is high partly because each board member called one-seventh of Pearton households, encouraging families to respond. The results show that 77 percent of families want more or much more homework, 25 percent want the same amount, and 4 percent want less.

Of the thirty-five rural superintendents interviewed, twenty-two discuss their homework policy (twenty say they have a policy to give homework, while two say they have a no-homework policy). Thirteen superintendents say that their districts leave homework up to teachers, with no formal homework policy; in those districts, teachers give their students homework.

The principal's report on library research about homework and student learning concludes that homework can enhance student learning when it provides opportunities to practice, outside of class, assignments that are discussed and reinforced in class. Thus, homework is effective when it fits integrally into the teacher's in-class lesson designs. That means homework facilitates learning when students see that it fits logically into what they do in class and when teachers use it to reinforce classroom presentations and discussion.

After several discussions about the data, the board members decide to hold two community meetings in which they tentatively advocate a prohomework policy.

Step 3: Distribute the Data and Announce Changes

Board members make another round of phone calls to Pearton families with children in school, inviting parents to attend either or both community meetings on homework. At the meetings, the superintendent presents data from step 2, and each board member states his or her advocacy for student homework. The board chairperson then

leads the audience in a question-and-answer session. Finally, the board members elicit ideas from parents about the quantity of homework that is reasonable. Both meetings end with the board announcing it will decide on a homework policy for Pearton at its next regular meeting.

Step 4: Try a New Practice

The Pearton school board passes a policy specifying that the teachers should assign homework to students regularly to enhance students' time on learning tasks integral to the teachers' lesson plans. The school board also announces its support for a series of three inservice training workshops for teachers, at which the details of the homework policy will be worked out.

Step 5: Check Others' Reactions

During the three inservice workshops, the principal documents how teachers feel about assigning homework to students. Virtually all teachers agree that having students practice assignments outside of class enhances student internalization of the teachers' lesson plans. After considerable discussion, the principal and the teachers decide that thirty minutes of homework in each subject should be assigned to all high school students on Mondays, Tuesdays, Wednesdays, and Thursdays and that once every three weeks, homework should be assigned to high school students on the weekend. With regard to elementary and middle school students, they decide that twenty minutes of homework in each subject should be assigned on school nights, but that the elementary and the middle school students should not be assigned homework on weekends. Later, at another community meeting, the principal presents details of the homework policy to parents.

Step 6: Collect Data

The following spring, about four months after the homework policy is in full swing, the school board launches data collections to assess how the homework policy is working. It asks the superintendent and the principal to write a questionnaire to measure teachers' perceptions and attitudes of the homework policy. That questionnaire includes a tailor-made matrix for each teacher. The matrix lists students' names vertically on the left side and academic subjects across the top. To fill out the cells in the matrix, each teacher uses a five-point scale:

5   Very high level of performance

4   High level of performance

3   Medium level of performance

2   Low level of performance

1   Very low level of performance

In an effort to gather parents' views, each board member conducts telephone interviews with eight parents, drawn at random, making a total of fifty-six parent interviews. During the fifteen-minute interviews, parents are asked about strengths and shortcomings of the homework policy, how it might be improved, and whether they want more, less, or the same amounts of homework for their children in the future. In general, the data indicate that the new homework policy is working well.

Whole School Faculty*

To engage an entire faculty in action research is logistically challenging. Some schoolwide innovations offer excellent opportunities for whole faculties to carry out self-study and cooperative reflection. Such an ideal opportunity arises at Lakeside High School when district-office administrators announce the school will move to a block schedule and give up the traditional seven periods of fifty minutes each. The block schedule has three periods of two hours each arranged in A and B days. A days are Monday, Wednesday, and Friday one week and Tuesday and Thursday the next; B days are Tuesday and Thursday one week and Monday, Wednesday, and Friday the next. The mandated change presents Lakeside faculty with an opportunity for schoolwide proactive action research.

Step 1: Try a New Practice

With only fifteen weeks to prepare for the block schedule, the Lakeside faculty sets aside one full

day and five half-days for inservice training. The principal and the department heads hire consultants from the county education unit and a nearby college of education.

The consultants divide the twenty-member faculty into ten critical-friendship pairs. They use the technique of probing conversation to help faculty members plan how to use two hours at a time with their students. As those conversations unfold, it becomes apparent that many faculty members wish to use more cooperative-learning strategies and group projects in their teaching. Thus, the principals and the department heads decide to use two of the five half-days on various group-investigation methods.

Step 2: Incorporate Hopes and Concerns

During the full day of inservice training, the principal and department heads lead the faculty in a discussion about hopes and concerns. One of the hopes is to devote more time to Hunter's (1982) ITIP lesson design. Hunter's classic ITIP lesson design calls for seven steps: 1) create an anticipatory set for new learning; 2) tell students what they will be learning and why it is important for them to learn it; 3) use diverse media to provide information about the objective; 4) present concrete examples of concepts, rules, or skills to be learned; 5) check to make certain that students are understanding what is being presented; 6) give tasks for practice, either in class or as homework, for individualized practice; and 7) summarize what has been presented in this lesson.

In subsequent inservice sessions, the Lakeside faculty carries out group problem solving on the four concerns. (See Figure 8.12 for the complete list of Hopes and Concerns of the Lakeside Faculty.)

Step 3: Collect Data

The principal and the department heads collect data from teachers during inservice training and from teachers and students during the first

All names of educators, schools, and communities have been changed.

Hopes and Concerns of the Lakeside Faculty

Hopes

- Students will learn more about each subject and perform better on statewide achievement tests by spending concentrated times on subjects

- Teachers will give more time to each of Hunter's ITIP seven steps, with more concentrated time to teach

- The students will experience a greater variety of teaching methods and, in particular, will become more engaged in teaching one another during cooperative-learning projects

- There will be more opportunities to give students feedback as they practice what they are being taught

Concerns

- We will need help in understanding how best to use two-hour periods for student learning

- More time could be wasted in off-task activities

- Some students won't be able to stay focused mentally on the subject for two hours

- Disruptive students could be more of a problem in block schedule than in the traditional fifty-minute period

Figure 8.12

semester of block scheduling. During inservice training, the principal and the department heads collect data to track the faculty's reactions and behavioral changes in three ways. Figure 8.13 explains the Three Ways Data Are Collected from Teachers.

The principal and the department heads meet once a week from October to December to make constructive changes in the inservice training sessions.

From February to June, while block scheduling is underway, the principal and the department heads form the ten pairs of faculty members into five groups of four each to get everyone to collect data about Lakeside's experiment with the new schedule.

One group of four presents a questionnaire on the seven steps of Hunter's (1982) ITIP for its colleagues to complete once every three weeks. With this first data set, the initiators want to remind their colleagues of the faculty's commitment to design lessons with ITIP in mind.

The second group of four creates interview statements to ask its colleagues how the block schedule does or does not facilitate student learning.

The third group administers a questionnaire to assess the students' attitudes toward block scheduling.

The fourth group prepares interview questions to measure students' reactions to the block schedule and chooses twenty students at random

Three Ways Data Are Collected from Teachers

1. The principal and the department heads ask teachers to fill out post-meeting reaction questionnaires about each inservice training. The post-meeting forms ask for helpful and unhelpful things about each session and for suggestions on how to improve future sessions.

2. The principal and the department heads interview three to four colleagues once every

two weeks about the transition to block scheduling.

3. The principal and the department heads each observes the faculty members' involvement in all activities during the inservice training. They note whether teachers construct concrete plans for the two-hour blocks of teaching and learning.

Figure 8.13

to interview in mid-May about how to improve the block schedule.

The fifth group observes classrooms in process, focusing on the teachers' use of different activity structures and the students' time on task in each activity structure. Finally, the principal and the department heads administer achievement tests to all students at the end of May. They compare these scores with students' achievement test scores from a year ago.

Step 4: Check What the Data Mean

The Lakeside faculty retreats for three days to check what the five sets of data mean. Each of the four-person data-collection teams presents its findings and interpretations to the faculty. The principal and department heads discuss the meanings they each derive from the data in a panel.

Step 5: Reflect on Alternative Ways to Behave

During the third day of its June conference, the faculty reflects on the next steps to refine block scheduling. Figure 8.14 defines the Key Points to Refine Block Scheduling.

Step 6: Try Another New Practice

During the summer, the principal prepares a class schedule that includes blocks in English, social studies, science, foreign language, and fine arts,

as well as fifty-minute daily periods in math and physical education. In August, the Lakeside faculty spends one day reflecting on step 5 and planning details of its orientation day with the students. Lakeside's new block schedule is on the way to becoming institutionalized.

Educator-Stakeholder Task Force*

The superintendent and the school board members wish to take stock of how Hamilton's citizens view their schools. They appoint a fifteen-member educator-stakeholder task force to execute the study. The superintendent asks the high school principal to chair the task force. To form the task force, the superintendent and the principal nominate seven teachers, while the seven board members each nominate one Hamilton citizen. The superintendent and the board members ask the task force to gather information to assess citizens' views about the district's strengths and shortcomings and to advise on policies to improve the schools' effectiveness in the community. The high school principal and one of the task force's teachers tell the task force about cooperative, responsive action research. They use the label "needs assessment" to commence the research, defining "needs" as current conditions in schools that should be improved.

Key Points to Refine Block Scheduling

- The faculty should receive more training in the seven steps of ITIP and in alternative ways to implement cooperative learning.

- Pairs of faculty members will design more two-hour blocks together.

- Some revision will be made in the class schedule so that math and physical education classes can be fifty minutes every day, rather than two hours every other day. All

other curriculum domains will continue with the block schedule.

- The faculty will spend the first day of school in September presenting students with an orientation to block scheduling. The orientation will include information about the faculty's aspirations for the program, its concerns about what might go wrong, and its up-to-date group agreements about how it plans to cope with the concerns.

Figure 8.14

All names of educators, schools, and communities have been changed.

Step 1: Collect Data

The task force decides to use telephone interviews to collect data. Two teachers volunteer to draw a random sample of 150 Hamilton citizens. Each task-force member agrees to interview ten citizens. Figure 8.15 lists the Three Open-Ended Interview Questions.

For more data, the task force uses content from interviews to prepare a structured questionnaire. The questionnaire has four sections:

- A list of ten strengths, each accompanied by a five-point Likert scale ranging from strongly agree to strongly disagree.
- A list of eight shortcomings, each with a five-point Likert scale.
- A list of eight conditions that should be improved, each accompanied by a three-point scale.
- A list of demographic questions, including queries about age, sex, and number of children in school.

For ease of analysis, the questionnaire is printed so that the answers can be mechanically scanned. It is mailed to every household in Hamilton.

Step 2: Analyze the Data

The results reveal that Hamilton's citizens agree on the schools' strengths, but they agree less on its shortcomings. Of the shortcomings that call for improvement, the four that are most important are the following:

- Ensuring student safety
- Engaging senior citizens more in school programs
- Upgrading facilities for handicapped access

- Modernizing computer systems in schools

The task force finds that 78 percent of the returned questionnaires were filled out by mothers with children in school. Many citizens without children in school did not return the questionnaire.

Step 3: Distribute the Data and Announce Changes

The task force holds community meetings to feed back data and collect more reactions from attendees. Since only thirty-five citizens attended the first meeting at the high school, task-force members decide to hold subsequent meetings in homes. They divide into pairs (one educator and one stakeholder in each pair) to run seven meetings throughout various neighborhoods in Hamilton. The discussions in people's homes bring out two more needs for change: opening the schools to community organizations and controlling student behaviors at evening sports events. The task force announces that it will make policy recommendations to the school board in a month.

Step 4: Try a New Practice

The task force makes its recommendations to the school board. Figure 8.16 outlines the Task Force Recommendations.

The school board acts on recommendations one and four by posing a bond issue and by establishing a policy that once every two years Hamilton citizens will be surveyed for their perceptions of needs for school improvement. The school board also asks the superintendent to organize strategies to work on recommendations two and three. In turn, the superintendent

Three Open-Ended Interview Questions

1. What do you see as strengths of Hamilton's schools?
2. What do you see as shortcomings of Hamilton's schools?
3. What conditions would you like to see improved in Hamilton's schools?

Figure 8.15

Task Force Recommendations

The task force makes four recommendations to the school board:

1. Initiate a bond issue to modernize the facilities for handicapped access and for the schools' computer systems.

2. Experiment with a community-school program so that more citizens without children in school can participate in school-sponsored programs.

3. Collaborate with Hamilton's police to enhance student safety and to control unruly student behavior at evening sports events.

4. Make this community assessment of needs for school improvement a regular and routine part of the district's program.

Figure 8.16

engages the administrative cabinet (principals, curriculum director, and business manager) in its own action research about the community-school concept. The administrative cabinet appoints a five-person committee of high school teachers to meet with the police about student safety and student behavior at evening sports events.

In relation to the community-school concept, the middle school staff agrees to try a model from Flint, Michigan, for the next few years. (The Flint schools remain open through the evening hours to sponsor educational and social programs for adults residing in the neighborhood of the school.) In relation to student safety, high school faculty members agree to address student safety as a problem-solving topic in social studies classes and to participate more actively with students at evening sports events.

Step 5: Check Others' Reactions

Each board member makes ten to fifteen phone calls to check citizens' reactions to the bond issue. With those data, the school board makes a few changes in the wording of the bond issue, offers it to the public for a vote, and wins the support of 54 percent of voters.

The administrative cabinet studies citizens' participation in the community-school program and determines whether citizens without children in school increase their participation.

The high school principal, along with department heads, collects data on complaints of students, teachers, and parents about safety and behavior at sports events.

Step 6: Collect Data

To follow the specific actions of the year, the school board holds a public meeting at the end of the school year to elicit citizens' reactions to 1) the community-school program at the middle school, 2) student safety in the schools, and 3) student behavior at evening sports events. At that meeting, the board members listen to citizens' statements, record points about which most participants agree, and ask all participants to complete a post-meeting reaction form on the effectiveness of the meeting procedures. At its next meeting, the school board announces that once every two years it will sponsor a survey of citizens' perceptions of the school districts' strengths, shortcomings, and needs for improvement.

Typical One-on-One Partnerships

Reflect on some of the one-on-one partnerships you've used in the past, you're currently using, or you could use in the future.

1. A teacher and a teacher

   Past:

   Present:

   Future:

2. A teacher and a student

   Past:

   Present:

   Future:

3. A counselor and a student

   Past:

   Present:

   Future:

4. An administrator and a teacher

   Past:

   Present:

   Future:

Typical Small Face-to-Face Groups

Reflect on some of the small face-to-face groups you've used in the past, you're currently using, or you could use in the future.

1. One educator (a teacher, a counselor, or an administrator) with a few students drawn from different classrooms and grade levels

   Past:

   Present:

   Future:

2. Collegial teams of teachers from different grade levels or diverse disciplines

   Past:

   Present:

   Future:

3. Mixed intraschool teams of teachers, counselors, specialists, and administrators with responsibility to represent their colleagues

   Past:

   Present:

   Future:

4. Site councils or intraschool governing teams with educators, classified staff members, and parents

   Past:

   Present:

   Future:

5. School boards from districts with diverse ethnic groups and people from all walks of life

   Past:

   Present:

   Future:

Whole School Staff Proactive Action Research

Reflect on some of the reasons your school has engaged in, is currently engaged in, or might engage in whole school staff proactive action research.

Past:

Present:

Future:

Whole School Staff Responsive Action Research

Reflect on some of the reasons your school has engaged in, is currently engaged in, or might engage in whole school staff responsive action research.

Past:

Present:

Future:

Educator-Stakeholder Task Forces

Reflect on some of the educator-stakeholder task forces your school has established, is currently establishing, or might establish.

Past:

Present:

Future:

Reflections

Reflect on chapter 8 by answering these questions:

1. For each case, list a few strengths and weaknesses.

Case	Strengths	Weaknesses
One-on-One Partnership		
One Educator with Students		
Collegial Teacher Team		
Mixed Educator Team		
Site Council		
School Board		
Whole School Faculty		
Educator-Stakeholder Task Force		

2. What aspects of the eight cases might work in your school district?

Chapter 9

Prominent Researchers

There is a striking kinship between Kurt Lewin and the work of John Dewey. Both agree that democracy must be learned anew in each generation and that it is a far more difficult form of social structure to attain and maintain than is autocracy. —Gordon Allport

The relationship between researchers and the researched has focused upon the benefit to the researcher and has treated the needs of people in the schools more or less as a nuisance . . . Quite aside from the morality of that older relationship, it has crippled efforts to make research useful to educators. —Philip Runkel

Allport, the social psychologist extraordinaire, pointed to Dewey's and Lewin's overlap of values in his foreword to Lewin's (1948) *Resolving Social Conflicts,* while years later my colleague, Phil Runkel (1978), reminds us that the conflict between action research and traditional social science dies hard.

Since Lewin's death in 1947, social scientists who publish about action research have been few and far between. The lion's share of modern Lewineans, particularly those with doctorates in psychology, publish some form of traditional social-science research. Even such action-oriented reformers as Warren Bennis, Lee Bradford, Kenneth Clark, Jack French, Jack Gibb, and Ron Lippitt published field studies primarily in traditional scholarly journals.

Nevertheless, following the ideological leadership of Dewey, Follett, and Lewin, a handful of social scientists and educators have contrib-

uted significantly to literature on action research and, more recently, to an emerging literature on teacher research. However, this small number of action researchers is dwarfed by the hundreds of traditional Lewineans, such as Morton Deutsch, Leon Festinger, Harold Kelly, Stanley Milgram, Stan Schachter, and John Thibault, who during the past fifty years have filled scholarly journals with creative research and illuminating theory.

John Dewey, Mary Parker Follett, and Kurt Lewin

Before discussing the contributions of action researchers, a few more words are in order about the conceptual hopes and democratic values of Dewey, Follett, and Lewin.

John Dewey

A high school and a university teacher, John Dewey (1859–1952) became America's best-known and most prolific educational philosopher. He considered democracy to be a quality of living together—a mode of community life—rather than only a form of government.

At the turn of the century, when members of diverse ethnic groups were coming together in the neighborhoods of Chicago and New York, Dewey conceptualized how to foster their cohesion and togetherness. He viewed public schooling, in particular, as a primary means for achieving social integration. Dewey argued that schooling should embody democracy in action, thereby serving as a microcosm and mirror of the larger democratic community.

Through democratic participation in classrooms, Dewey believed that students would learn concepts, values, and skills of cooperative living. He thought that group projects in which students cooperate to reflect on and study social issues or community problems would offer an important means for achieving a more democratic community.

Dewey's ideas about group projects resembled teacher-student and student-student cooperative action research. He argued, too, that teachers and administrators should work together democratically, not only because it is a moral way to run a school, but also because students could observe adults modeling democratic norms and procedures.

Mary Parker Follett

An author of four books and a popular lecturer on workplace democracy, Mary Parker Follett (1868–1933) sought the use of scientific methods to transform worker-manager conflict into creative solutions to enhance productivity. Like Dewey, she considered democracy as modes of daily social interaction rather than just a distant form of government. She believed that conflict in industrial organizations is natural and inevitable and argued that intergroup conflict can be harnessed to increase organizational effectiveness. She told audiences, "All polishing is done by friction" (Follett 1940, p.31). Follett argued that

workers and managers should bring their differences to joint conferences, where they could use scientific methods to resolve conflicts together.

Follett conceptualized four critical steps for workers and managers to achieve a creative and harmonious relationship. The key concept for her was "coordination." First is coordination by virtue of frequent face-to-face meetings of responsible parties. Second is coordination of participants to specify and define problems they have in common. Third is coordination of participants studying all aspects of problems together. Fourth is coordination of continual intergroup problem solving (Follett 1940). Note the similarity between Follett's ideas about coordination and the action-research steps.

Kurt Lewin

Kurt Lewin (1890–1947) is the father of action research. He emigrated from Germany in 1933 because, as a Jew, he could not qualify for a tenured professorship at the University of Berlin. The discrimination and prejudice he observed throughout his early years in Central Europe, along with the frightening rise of Nazism, motivated him to look for ways that social science could help strengthen democracy and reduce prejudice. Lewin saw action research as a means to democracy; indeed, at times Lewin thought of action research and democratic participation as synonymous.

During his all-too-brief fourteen years in the United States, he attracted dozens of outstanding students and coworkers to collaborate with him at Cornell, in Iowa, and at the Massachusetts Institute of Technology. Although he sought to integrate traditional science with action research, his collaborators spent most of their time and effort publishing traditional research in lieu of action research. It is surmised that the reason was (and still is) that promotion to full professor requires publication of traditional research in scholarly journals.

Even Lewin published his research primarily in scholarly journals. A notable exception was the book *Resolving Social Conflicts* (1948), which was edited by his wife, Gertrud Weiss Lewin, one year after his death. That collection of Lewin's work includes a few examples of his efforts at community-based action research during the years of World War II.

Lewin was dedicated and hardworking. He had time for every collaborator and was enormously influential in interpersonal exchanges. Many of his students and coworkers undoubtedly carried out a good deal of unpublished action research as consultants and social activists. Lewin truly believed in the value of human interdependence and sought to build bridges between practitioners and scientists.

Alice Miel and Stephen Corey

Alice Miel and Stephen Corey, two pioneers in linking action research to school improvement, both worked at the Horace-Mann-Lincoln Institute of School Experimentation at Columbia University, New York. Miel applied action research to classroom improvement, while Corey focused more on cooperative action research in schools and throughout districts.

Alice Miel

From 1944 to 1950, Alice Miel cooperated with Ken Benne (who worked with Lewin), Chandas Reid, and Alice Stewart in the Horace-Mann-Lincoln Institute of School Experimentation at Columbia University in New York. They used action-research methods to help elementary school teachers use cooperative-learning procedures in their classrooms. Miel and her associates consulted with over 100 teachers nationwide in one of the largest efforts ever to disseminate action-research methods.

The project's teachers planned cooperative-learning activities in small collegial groups for their students. They tried particular cooperative procedures in their own classes, collected systematic data about the processes and their effects, modified the cooperative procedures when needed, and collected additional data to track results. Miel and her associates taught teachers to

collect data in several ways and from several sources. The teachers amassed introspective data by keeping reflective journals about their teaching. They also collected perceptual and attitudinal data from their students, and their colleagues collected data on classroom behaviors of students during cooperative learning. The teachers also collected data from parents about their reactions to cooperative-learning activities.

Miel and her associates helped teachers reflect on the data, arranged for small groups of teachers to discuss the data, and facilitated group problem solving about ways to improve cooperative-learning activities. As the project unfolded, Miel and her associates taught teachers how to find scientific evidence for student growth in helpfulness, friendliness, independence, responsibility, and group skills. They also helped teachers collect data on students' cognitive growth and academic achievement in different curriculum domains. The project helped establish action research and cooperative learning as core parts of curriculum for graduate students at the Teachers College at Columbia (Miel et al. 1952).

Stephen Corey

Partly because of Miel's innovative efforts, Stephen Corey, then executive director of the Horace-Mann-Lincoln Institute of School Experimentation, organized three national conferences on action research to improve school practices. At one of those meetings, a group of school administrators from Denver, Colorado, took special interest in action research and subsequently cooperated with Corey and the staff of the institute to conceptualize action research from the point of view of school administration.

The Denver group distinguished between empirical action research and the more typical casual inquiry, which group members thought most school administrators do every day. Using empirical action research, data are systematically sought, recorded, and interpreted to discover any problems (as in responsive action research) and to learn the effect of using new procedures to solve existing problems (as in proactive action research).

The Denver group wanted to answer whether a particular action truly did result in desirable consequences. Group members labeled their question the action hypothesis. An action hypothesis of interest to high school principals in the Denver group was that high school curriculum committees comprising volunteers will be more productive than curriculum committees comprising appointees. The group also wished to collect data on undesirable outcomes that might accompany the expected results. The principals deliberately searched for dysfunctional outcomes, such as colleagues feeling alienated from an elite group of volunteers. Corey's group, like Miel's teachers, sought multiple-method data from multiple sources.

After eight years of cooperative action-research projects throughout the United States, Corey (1953) came up with six conditions that foster effective school-based action research. His conditions are as true today as they were fifty years ago. See Figure 9.1 for Corey's Six Conditions that Foster Effective School-Based Action Research.

Ron Lippitt

Ron Lippitt, Lewin's student who did the most to nurture the development of action research, began working with Lewin in 1936. Although Lippitt was just twenty-four when he joined Lewin in Iowa City, he had already spent a year studying with Jean Piaget in Geneva, Switzerland. Lewin, Lippitt, and White finished the famous democratic, autocratic, laissez-faire leadership study of boys' clubs in 1939. With the start of World War II, Lewin's and Lippitt's research efforts turned to the societal needs and practical problems of that era.

During the 1950s, Lippitt taught planned change in the Research Center on Group Dynamics at the University of Michigan. In 1958, with students Jeanne Eisenstadt Watson and Bruce Westley, Lippitt wrote *The Dynamics of Planned Change* (1958). Although the term action research seldom appears, the book does outline the essential steps of responsive action research. Lippitt and his coauthors describe seven phases of planned change. Figure 9.2 outlines the Seven Phases of Planned Change.

Paulo Freire

Paulo Freire, an educational reformer, developed a radically innovative strategy of adult learning and social change during the 1960s in Brazil and in Chile. Freire likened traditional education to a bank where teachers deposit knowledge into students who serve as depositories. The proper role of a student is to receive, to file, to store, and, when called upon, to issue the deposits (Freire 1970).

Corey's Six Conditions that Foster Effective School-Based Action Research

1. *Openness to Weakness:* Administrators and staff members speak honestly to one another about those parts of the school program that need improvement.

2. *Chances for Creativity:* Administrators provide staff members with opportunities to brainstorm and analyze inventive ideas about alternative future practices.

3. *Support for Trial and Error:* Administrators provide staff members with support, resources, and materials to initiate and test alternative practices.

4. *Cooperative Staff Relations:* Administrators and staff members share norms and skills that support cooperative problem solving about their own group efforts.

5. *Value Data Collection:* Administrators and staff members believe they should go beyond casual inquiry to collect systematic data about their processes and school outcomes.

6. *Time for Improvement:* Administrators create ways to release staff members from regular duties to become engaged in professional reflection, action research, and staff problem solving.

Figure 9.1

Seven Phases of Planned Change

Phase 1: An individual or team pinpoints a need for change. Although the need for change might emanate from frustration, the individual or team strives to define the need as a current situation falling short of a target or ideal state.

Phase 2: Systematic data are collected about the current situation and the participants' wishes for the ideal state. The data come from multiple sources.

Phase 3: The data are used to create a diagnosis of the situation. This phase can include the Force-Field Analysis (see chapter 1), which Lewin conceptualized as part of his field theory.

Phase 4: After the diagnosis, a plan is made to change the current situation and move toward the ideal state. This phase is the heart of planned change; it must be guided by data for it to be action research.

Phase 5: The plans of phase 4 are converted into actual change efforts—these efforts are the actions of action research.

Phase 6: The actions are assessed. (Are the change efforts working?) Systematic data are collected.

Phase 7: The best parts of the actions are institutionalized.

Figure 9.2

While teaching illiterate adults to read and to feel empowered to change their impoverished lives, Freire thought of teaching and learning as a mutually interactive exchange—learners teach and learn at the same time. Adult development occurs in groups. The group process of learning together is organized around creative problem solving, during which participants reflect on their situations. At the same time, participants are learning to read. The psychological keys to learning to read are reflection about oneself, discussion about others' reflections, and cooperation with peers to change things for the better. Reading, reflecting, feeling empowered, and cooperating to solve problems cannot be separated.

Just as professional reflection is linked to action research, self-reflection is linked to actively improving one's own situation. Although Freire writes very little about systematic data collections in his pedagogical strategy, his stress on interpersonal dialogue assumes that it is through open and honest exchanges of personal information—or as we have called it, probing conversation—that adult learners grow. People grow intellectually and emotionally when they grapple with the thoughts, feelings, and skills of others. In that sense, Freire views dialogue as exchanges of data to help participants improve their own lives.

Chris Argyris and Donald Schön

Chris Argyris and Donald Schön are both action scientists, a variation of action researchers. Action scientists study what social-psychological dynamics are present in a concrete social situation. They review published research that might shed light on that particular situation, plan strategies to change the status quo, intervene to improve the status quo, evaluate how improvements unfold and interrelate, plan revised strategies and interventions, and then continually plan, intervene, and evaluate. As these cycles of action and research play out, action scientists strive to create general principles and hypotheses that serve as building blocks of scientific theories of planned social change.

Chris Argyris

Chris Argyris created action science with Harvard University students during the seventies and early eighties. In action science, a bundle of interrelated intellectual and behavioral events produce 1) concrete data for local action, problem solving, and improvement and 2) general principles for scientific theories of planned change. Like Lewin, Argyris hoped to build bridges between practical action researchers and theoretical social scientists (Argyris, Putnam, and Smith 1985).

Many traditional social scientists believe that their knowledge contributes to the work of action researchers; however, they often do not believe that knowledge gleaned from local action research contributes to development of more general theory. Argyris, like Lewin, does not agree. Argyris argues that traditional social scientists can learn a great deal by studying how action researchers go about changing things. He offers Lewin's Force-Field Analysis (see chapter 1) as a case in point.

Donald Schön

Donald Schön (1983 and 1987), Arygris's colleague at Harvard, contributed to our understanding of how professional reflection can facilitate improved practice. Schön sees reflective practice engaging teachers, administrators, or students in cycles of introspection and action, based on their experiences in the classroom and in the school. During reflection, according to Schön, mature professionals think critically about their plans, decisions, actions, and effects on others to improve them tomorrow, next week, or next month. As educators introspect about their past and present actions, they create concepts, hopes, and concerns to guide their future actions.

Schön writes about reflection on action and reflection in action. Reflection on action entails thinking critically about one's actions after they have had an effect (e.g., reflecting on one's achievements and failures with a particular lesson plan). Reflection in action entails thinking critically about one's actions in the midst of action (e.g., reflecting on others' reactions to a lesson being taught). Schön's two types of reflection offer data, in the style of a personal action-research project, to plan for future changes. The art of personal and group reflection about past, present, and future events are integral processes of action research.

Stephen Kemmis and Jean McNiff

Stephen Kemmis and Jean McNiff, prominent proponents of action research in the 1980s, did most of their work in England. More recently, Kemmis has been facilitating school-based action research in Australia.

Stephen Kemmis

Taking cues from Schön, Stephen Kemmis's primary concern is in helping teachers critically reflect on their practice. He is more concerned with teacher introspection and teacher-teacher dialogue about practice than he is with the collection of systematic data, at least in the sense of using questionnaires, interviews, or documents. Kemmis's main research method is teachers making critical observations of their own practice (Kemmis and McTaggart 1988).

In *The Action Research Planner,* Kemmis and McTaggart (1988) delineate their self-reflective cycle—plan, act, observe, reflect, and plan, act, observe, reflect, etc. For an example of the Self-Reflective Cycle, see Figure 9.3.

Self-Reflective Cycle

A teacher realizes she is unhappy with student involvement in social studies (planning). Although she cannot change the prescribed curriculum, she can change how students work within the curriculum. She decides to use helping trios in social studies instruction. The teacher explains to students how helping trios work, and she forms students into trios (acting). Next, she listens in on a few trios to assess how they are going (observing). She is pleased with student energy and involvement, but she is worried about too little student time on task (reflecting). The teacher decides to train students in how to use a structured interview within trios (planning). She carries out the training (acting). Then, she listens in on a few trios (observing). She likes what is happening in general (observing); however, she is concerned about four of her special-needs students who are not as highly involved as the other students. Thus, self-reflective cycles of personal action research continue.

Figure 9.3

Jean McNiff

Jean McNiff has extended Corey's, Lippitt's, and Kemmis's work in educational action research. In her book *Action Research: Principles and Practice,* McNiff (1988) describes the conceptual and historical bases of action research. She outlines how to start an action-research project and describes various data-collection techniques that are readily available to teachers.

McNiff urges educators to start small when they initiate their first action-research project. Teachers or administrators should start with their own personal, small-scale projects, or teachers and administrators should start with cooperative action research that is narrowly focused. McNiff stresses careful and deliberate planning, a realistic timetable for data collection, careful involvement of key stakeholders, and the establishment of clear and open communication with relevant administrators. Her book is replete with case studies of action research and includes tips on how to establish a collaborative network of action researchers.

William Foote Whyte

In 1991, William Foote Whyte edited *Participatory Action Research,* which presents case studies of action research in industry and in agriculture. Whyte's text does not give information about educational action research. Names like Dewey, Follett, Lewin, Miel, Corey, Lippitt, and Freire are notably absent from it, but Whyte's book adds to the understanding of the multiple roots of action research.

Whyte argues that action research in industry and in agriculture flows out of three intellectual streams in social science. Figure 9.4 explains these three intellectual streams.

Richard Sagor

Richard Sagor's *How to Conduct Collaborative Action Research,* published in 1992 by the Association for Supervision and Curriculum Development (ASCD), is a small but impressive text. It presents background information on why educa-

Whyte's Intellectual Streams

1. *The participatory research methods of social anthropologists and sociologists.* Participatory research methods, such as participant observation, have not been popular in psychology, where questionnaires, interviews, and documents often prevail. Whyte emphasizes observations made by participants themselves (e.g., group members serving as process observers, individual participants keeping journals about their own experiences, and nonparticipants watching action-research participants throughout different phases of action research).

2. *The participation of lower-echelon workers in organizational decision making.* Whyte refers to innovations aimed at democratizing the workplace, such as organizational development, total quality management, and quality of work-life programs. He argues that once workers participate with management in decision making, the idea of active coopera-

tion between management and labor in a research process becomes legitimate. In that sense, Whyte views the rise of action research as depending on previous acceptance of worker participation in administrative matters.

3. *The concept that worker behavior depends on a combination of cultural and technological variables.* Whyte refers to the one-sided nature of Frederick Taylor's technocratic strategy of scientific management. Whyte argues that as scientific managers were influenced by the human relations movement to seek an integration between the human side and the technical side of the workplace, they could also recognize the benefit of engaging workers in action research to improve productivity. Thus, what has come to be called sociotechnical theory lends intellectual support to the idea of participatory action research.

Figure 9.4

tors need cooperative action research, what it is, and how to put it into a school or district.

Sagor offers five sequential steps, which are similar to the first four steps of responsive action research. Figure 9.5 highlights the five steps.

Another helpful aspect of Sagor's book is the practical information he gives about the three data sets mentioned in step 2.

Teacher Research

The historical trend from Dewey, Follett, and Lewin to Kemmis, McNiff, and Sagor is in the direction of making action research more and more accessible to busy, overloaded teachers and administrators. The more recent researchers work as partners in the trenches. They write about practical, down-to-earth research methods that can readily be applied to real classrooms and schools. They also seek to establish educator networks so that colleagues can support one another in doing what has become known as teacher research.

Sagor's Five Sequential Steps

1. *A problem of great concern is defined and analyzed.* Borrowing from the creative work of Peter Holly and Gene Southworth (1989), Sagor describes how to use graphic flow-charts to depict interconnected parts of an educational problem.

2. *Data are collected about the problem.* Sagor argues that at least three data sets (existing data, methods to assess everyday life, and questioning methods) should be gathered for each problem. The first data set concerns records that already exist, such as student files, attendance data, teacher records about student behavior, and portfolios of student work. The second set, methods to assess everyday life, includes student and teacher journals, audio or video recordings of classroom activities, visitors' perceptions and reactions, systematic observations (both structured and unstructured), and photo-graphs of classroom activity structures and of students in various school settings outside the classroom. The third set, questioning methods, includes individual and focus-group interviews, paper-and-pencil question-naires (including sociometric inventories), and achievement tests.

3. *The data are analyzed for themes and patterns.* Sagor presents the idea of a data matrix as a useful device for organizing data and pinpointing themes.

4. *The results of the data analysis are reported to significant stakeholders.* Sagor gives helpful ideas on how to structure the report.

5. *A plan for action is prepared and imple-mented.* Sagor advocates using Lewin's Force-Field Analysis (see chapter 1) to develop action plans.

Figure 9.5

Reflections

Reflect on chapter 9 by answering these questions:

1. Which two prominent researchers do you relate to most closely? Explain the reasons.

2. Which four ideas of these thirteen prominent researchers would you like to incorporate into your own repertoire as an action researcher?

3. How might you like to contribute to the teacher-research movement?

Afterword

Teacher research is classroom-based action research implemented by teachers, published by teachers, and disseminated from teacher to teacher for the education and the enrichment of teachers. It has grown in Australia, England, and the United States. Stephen Kemmis and Robert McTaggart in Australia; Peter Holly, Jean McNiff, and Robert Stenhouse in England; and Sandra Hollingsworth, Ruth Hubbard, and Brenda Power in the United States have lead in creating this new discipline, a living body of work that resonates with Dewey's vision of a more democratic social science (Dewey 1916; Hollingsworth 1994).

The new discipline of teacher research, particularly as Hubbard and Power conceive it, is being fueled by intellectual analyses of three contemporary reform movements in education. First is the constructivist (as opposed to the positivist) position that classroom teachers can create a valid knowledge base about teaching and learning. In reality, they build theory and do research everyday in their own classrooms. We should codify and legitimize those efforts. Second is the critical-theory (as opposed to the elitist

social science) position that classroom teachers, who have been powerless and silent about educational theory and research, have an important contribution to make in producing knowledge about teaching and learning. Third is the feminist (as opposed to a male-dominated social science) position that classroom teachers (mostly women) and children (the students) can contribute to a more comprehensive and humane theory that explains how teaching and learning operate in classrooms.

In the fall of 1993, Hubbard and Power edited volume 1, number 1 of *Teacher Research: The Journal of Classroom Inquiry.* The contributions, mostly case studies by teachers about their own classrooms, report on action-research projects and special efforts at self-reflection and critical self-analysis to solve student problems. With the appearance of this journal, the conceptual wishes of Dewey, Follett, Lewin, and Lippitt come alive. With the efforts of Hollingsworth, Hubbard, Power, and Sagor, those old conceptual wishes are becoming current practical realities.

Bibliography

Argyris, C., R. Putnam, and D. M. Smith. 1985. *Action science.* San Francisco: Jossey-Bass.

Aronson, E. 1978. *The jigsaw classroom.* Beverly Hills: Sage Publications.

Berman, P. and M. McLaughlin. 1975. *Federal programs supporting educational change.* Vol. 6, *The findings in review.* Santa Monica, Calif.: Rand Corporation.

Bradford, L., J. Gibb, and K. Benne, eds. 1964. *T-group theory and laboratory method.* New York: John Wiley and Sons.

Coch, L. and J. French. 1948. Overcoming resistance to change. *Human Relations,* 4: 512–32.

Corey, S. M. 1953. *Action research to improve school practices.* New York: Bureau of Publications, Teachers College, Columbia University.

Dewey, J. 1916. *Democracy and Education.* New York: The Free Press.

———. 1933. *How we think.* Boston: Heath.

———. 1939. *Intelligence in the modern world: John Dewey's philosophy,* edited by J. Ratner. New York: The Modern Library.

Follett, M. P. 1924. *Creative experience.* New York: Longman's.

———. 1940. *Dynamic administration.* New York: Harper & Brothers.

———. 1965. *The new state: Group organization, the solution of popular government.* 2d ed. Gloucester, Mass.: Peter Smith.

Fox, R., M. Luszki, and R. A. Schmuck. 1966. *Diagnosing classroom learning environments.* Chicago, Ill.: Science Research Associates.

Freire, P. 1970. *Pedagogy of the oppressed.* New York: Herder & Herder.

Hall, G. E. and S. M. Hord. 1987. *Change in schools: Facilitating the process.* Albany, N.Y.: State University of New York Press.

Hess, R. T. 1996. *Writing process, portfolios, and programs: Teacher action research.* Unpublished master's thesis, Oregon State University, Corvallis, Oregon.

Hollingsworth, S. 1994. *Teacher research and urban literacy education: Lessons and conversations in a feminist key.* New York: Teachers College Press.

Holly, P. and G. Southworth. 1989. *The developing school.* London: Falmer Press.

Hubbard, R. and B. Power, eds. 1993. *Teacher research: The journal of classroom inquiry,* Vol. 1, no. 1. Fall 1993. Orono, Maine: University of Maine.

Hunter, M. 1982. *Mastery teaching.* El Segundo, Calif.: Instructional Dynamics.

Kanter, R. 1983. *The changemasters.* New York: Simon and Schuster.

Kemmis, S. and R. McTaggart. 1988. *The action research planner.* 3d ed. Victoria, Australia: Deakin University Press.

Kohl, H. R. 1969. *The open classroom: A practical guide to a new way of teaching.* New York: New York Review Book.

Leary, W. G. and J. S. Smith, eds. 1951. *Think before you write.* New York: Harcourt, Brace and Co.

Lewin, K. 1948. *Resolving social conflicts.* New York: Harpers.

———. 1951. *Field theory in social psychology.* New York: Harpers.

Lippitt, P. and J. Lohman. 1965. Cross-age relationships: An educational resource. *Children,* 12: 113–17.

Lippitt, P., J. Eisman, and R. Lippitt. 1969. *Cross-age helping programs: Orientation, training, and related materials.* Ann Arbor: University of Michigan's Center for Research on Utilization of Scientific Knowledge, Institute for Social Research.

Lippitt, R. 1949. *Training in community relations: Toward new group skills.* New York: Harper & Brothers.

Lippitt, R., J. E. Watson, and B. Westley. 1958. *The dynamics of planned change.* New York: Harcourt, Brace, and Co.

Marrow, A. J. 1969. *The practical theorist: The life and work of Kurt Lewin.* New York: Basic Books.

McNiff, J. 1988. *Action research: Principles and practice.* London: Macmillan Education.

Mead, G. H. 1934. *Mind, self, and society.* Chicago, Ill.: University of Chicago Press.

Mead, M. 1953. *Growing up in New Guinea.* New York: Mentor Books.

Miel, A., et al. 1952. *Cooperative procedures in learning.* New York: Bureau of Publications, Teachers College, Columbia University.

Miles, M. B. 1981. *Learning to work in groups.* 2d ed. New York: Teachers College Press, Columbia University.

Moreno, J. L. 1953. *Who shall survive.* New York: Beacon House.

Robertson, E. 1992. Is Dewey's educational vision still viable? In *Review of research in education,* edited by G. Grant. Washington, D.C.: American Educational Research Association.

Runkel, P. 1978. A consultant's view of research methods. In *Social psychology of education: Theory and research,* edited by D. Bar-Tal and L. Saxe. Washington, D.C.: Hemisphere.

Sagor, R. 1992. *How to conduct collaborative action research.* Alexandria, Va.: Association of Supervision and Curriculum Development.

Sarason, S. 1990. *The predictable failure of educational reform.* San Francisco: Jossey-Bass.

Schmuck, R. A. 1968. Helping teachers improve classroom group processes. *Journal of Applied Behavioral Science* 4: 401–35.

Schmuck, R. A., M. Chesler, and R. Lippitt. 1966. *Problem solving to improve classroom learning.* Chicago, Ill.: Science Research Associates.

Schmuck, R. A., and P. Runkel. 1994. *The handbook of organization development in schools and colleges.* 4th ed. Prospect Heights, Ill.: Waveland Press.

Schmuck, R. A., and P. Schmuck. 1997. *Group processes in the classroom.* 7th ed. Madison, Wis.: Brown and Benchmark.

Schön, D. 1983. *The reflective practitioner.* New York: Basic Books.

———. 1987. *Educating the reflective practitioner: Toward a new design for teaching and learning in the professions.* San Francisco: Jossey-Bass.

Scriven, M. 1980. *The logic of evaluation.* Inverness, Calif.: Edgepress.

Sharan, Y. and S. Sharan. 1992. *Expanding cooperative learning through group investigation.* New York: Teachers College Press.

Sizer, T. R. 1984. *Horace's compromise: The dilemma of the American high school.* Boston: Houghton Mifflin.

———. 1992. *Horace's compromise: Redesigning the American high school.* Boston: Houghton Mifflin.

Stringer, E. T. 1996. *Action research: A handbook for practitioners.* Thousand Oaks, Calif.: Sage Publications.

Thelen, H. 1981. *The classroom society.* New York: Harsted Press.

Walker, R. 1985. *Doing research: A handbook for teachers.* London: Methuen & Co.

Whyte, W. F. 1943. *Street corner society.* Chicago, Ill.: University of Chicago Press.

———, ed. 1991. *Participatory action research.* Newbury Park, Calif.: Sage Publications.

IRI/SkyLight Training and Publishing, Inc.

Index

Notes

Notes

Notes

Notes

Notes

Notes

SkyLight
Training and Publishing Inc.

We Prepare Your Teachers Today
for the Classrooms of Tomorrow

Learn from Our Books and from Our Authors!

Ignite Learning in Your School or District.

SkyLight's team of classroom-experienced consultants can help you foster systemic change for increased student achievement.

Professional development is a process, not an event. SkyLight's seasoned practitioners drive the creation of our on-site professional development programs, graduate courses, research-based publications, interactive video courses, teacher-friendly training materials, and online resources—call SkyLight Training and Publishing Inc. today.

SkyLight specializes in three professional development areas.

Specialty #
1
Best Practices

We **model** the best practices that result in improved student performance and guided applications.

Specialty #
2
Making the Innovations Last

We help set up **support** systems that make innovations part of everyday practice in the long-term systemic improvement of your school or district.

Specialty #
3
How to Assess the Results

We prepare your school leaders to encourage and **assess** teacher growth, **measure** student achievement, and **evaluate** program success.

Contact the SkyLight team and begin a process toward long-term results.

SkyLight
Training and Publishing Inc.

2626 S. Clearbrook Dr., Arlington Heights, IL 60005
800-348-4474 • 847-290-6600 • FAX 847-290-6609
http://www.iriskylight.com

There are

one-story intellects,

two-story intellects, and three-story

intellects with skylights. All fact collectors, who

have no aim beyond their facts, are one-story men. Two-story men

compare, reason, generalize, using the labors of the fact collectors as

well as their own. Three-story men idealize, imagine,

predict—their best illumination comes from

above, through the skylight.

—*Oliver Wendell*

Holmes

SkyLight
Training and Publishing Inc.